IS 61 LIBRARY

I REMEMBER
the ALAMO

D. ANNE LOVE

A YEARLING BOOK

Published by
Dell Yearling
an imprint of
Random House Children's Books
a division of Random House, Inc.
1540 Broadway
New York, New York 10036

The trademarks Yearling® and Dell® are registered in the U.S. Patent and
Trademark Office and in other countries.

Visit us on the Web! www.randomhouse.com/kids

Educators and librarians, for a variety of teaching tools, visit us at
www.randomhouse.com/teachers

ISBN: 0-440-41697-3

Reprinted by arrangement with Holiday House, Inc.

Printed in the United States of America

May 2001

10 9 8 7 6 5 4 3

OPM

*This book is dedicated
to the children of Texas, past and present,
and to the memory of the men
of the Alamo
—D.A.L.*

CONTENTS

1.	Gone to Texas	1
2.	The Travelers	9
3.	Velasco	21
4.	Angelina	34
5.	The Texian	43
6.	The Promise	56
7.	Thirteen Days	65
8.	Remember the Alamo	77
9.	Santa Anna	88
10.	The Runaway Scrape	101
11.	An Unexpected Encounter	120
12.	Jessie's Choice	128
13.	Pa's Gift	142
14.	Another Journey	151
15.	A Place to Call Home	162
	A Brief Texas Chronology	166
	Author's Note	169

1

GONE *to* TEXAS

One afternoon toward the end of October, Jessie McCann looked up from her family's wash to see a horse and rider coming through the trees. She dropped the stick she was using to stir the clothes and raced along the dirt path, bursting into her cabin flushed and breathless.

"Mama! Yancy! Pa's coming!"

Mama looked up from her spinning wheel. "I don't think so, dear. It's too soon."

Yancy came in, his arms loaded with firewood. At fifteen, he was taller than Pa and almost as strong. He grinned at Jessie. "What happened? I heard you yelling clear out to the woodpile."

"Pa's coming. I saw him riding up the road."

"See who it is, son," Mama said calmly.

Yancy looked out. "It *is* Pa! Come on, Jess!"

1

Pa rode up, his saddlebags bulging. He leapt from the saddle and swept Mama into the air.

"Luther!" she cried. "Put me down!" But she was laughing right along with him. "What on earth are you doing back here? I thought you were going to Smathers' Bluff."

"Plans changed. Let's go in and I'll tell you about it. Where's Tad?"

"Here I am, Pa!" Tad launched himself into Pa's arms. "I thought you weren't coming back till Saturday. What did you bring me? A silver whistle?"

"Something better than a whistle," Pa said, setting Tad down. "Is there any coffee, Ruth? I'm plumb wore out."

While Mama made coffee, Jessie cooked Pa's eggs just the way he liked them. They all sat at the table while Pa ate. All but two-year-old Callie, who was sound asleep in her crib.

When his plate was clean, Pa pushed it away. Mama poured more coffee. Then Pa said, "Guess who I met on the way to Smathers' Bluff?"

"Davy Crockett!" Tad said.

"No," Pa said, his brown eyes full of laughter. "Guess again."

"President Jackson!" Jessie guessed.

"Oh, I hope not!" Mama said. "Not with you in those tatty old clothes, Luther."

Pa laughed. "Andy Jackson's not much for appearances himself, Ruth. But no, I didn't see Old Hickory."

He tipped his chair back. "On the way to Smathers' Bluff, I met two Texians. Finest fellows you'd ever want to meet. They say folks down there are about ready to declare their independence from Mexico. And there's thousands of acres of prime land to be had at bargain prices."

Jessie shot Yancy a sideways look.

"I know what you're thinking," Pa said. "But these fellows said Texas is chock-full of great rivers and green rolling prairies. Not rocky like Kentucky. Why, that land is so rich a man can practically plow it with his bare hands. Just think, Ruth, what we could do with a farm like that."

"But we're settled here now," Mama said. "The children have a school, and you have your shop."

"A *tinker's* shop," Pa scoffed.

"You may think it's nothing, but folks depend on you all the same," Mama declared. "Who would fix their tools and clocks, if not for you?"

"Well, from now on, they'll be depending on that Hallet fellow from over on Alton's Creek."

"What?"

"It was getting to me, Ruth. Sitting there every day fiddling with broken-down tools, while the whole big world was rushing by outside. So, after those two Texians rode off, I went and talked to Hallet. You know he's been after me to sell for more'n a year now."

"Oh, Pa!" Jessie cried. "You didn't!"

"Yes, ma'am, I surely did!" Pa's laughter rumbled like

mountain thunder. "Put everything I wanted into my two saddlebags and came straight home. This time next week, we'll be halfway to Texas."

"Texas?" Tad jumped up, tipping his chair over. Callie woke up and began to cry.

"I'll get her, Mama." Jessie was so angry, she was glad for any reason to leave the table. Why couldn't she have been born into a normal family? She must be the only girl in Kentucky, probably in the whole world, who had moved three times before turning twelve years old.

First they'd moved to the cabin on Washburn Creek. She was only four then and too young to go to school, but she'd had Yancy for a playmate. He was eight back then and knew about a million ways to have fun. Later there was Tad, and her sister Mary, before Mary got sick and went to heaven. Jessie didn't remember much about how their cabin looked. What she remembered was feelings. Happiness listening to Mama singing hymns as she spread the wash out to dry on the lilac bushes. Fear when afternoon thunder rolled across the mountains and shook their cabin the way a hound dog shakes a rabbit. Worry the year Pa's crops failed and there was no food to eat. After that, they moved to Cutter's Gap. Pa said life was better there anyway.

It was, and it wasn't. There was a school and Jessie went there with Yancy when she was seven. That was good. But then Pa started a turkey farm. Everybody else raised apples or tobacco, cows or pigs. But not Pa. He said turkeys were the future and would make them rich.

4

The other children in Miss Hunter's school made gobbling sounds every time Jessie or Yancy stood up to recite. They flapped their arms like turkeys' wings and called Yancy "Turkey Boy" instead of his rightful name.

When the turkeys sickened and died, Pa loaded the wagon and they moved here, to the cabin on Hickory Creek. Pa opened a shop in the settlement down the river. Once a month, he rode through the neighboring towns, stopping to fix whatever had broken since his last trip.

Now he was plucking his whole family up again, like weeds in a garden, and carting them off to Texas, all because of some strangers he'd met on the road.

"Come here, Callie," Jessie crooned. "Don't cry."

At the sight of her sister, Callie's tears stopped. Holding out her chubby arms, she grinned at Jessie, showing her tiny teeth. "Play, Jessie!"

"Not now," Jessie said. "Pa's talking. Come sit with me."

But Callie squirmed out of Jessie's arms and raced around the table to Yancy's chair. "You play!" she ordered, a tiny golden princess in a rumpled pinafore.

Pa scooped her up and tossed her into the air until Callie squealed. "Here's my girl. Give your old papa a kiss."

Callie planted noisy kisses on both of Pa's cheeks. He tucked her into his lap and went on talking.

"It won't be an easy trip," he said. "But it's the opportunity we've been waiting for. The chance of a lifetime.

5

How many men get to start up a brand-new country and buy themselves a fine farm in the bargain? I'm telling you, Ruth, this is the answer to our prayers. I can feel it in my bones!" He looked around the table at all of them, his eyes shining. This was Pa the way Jessie knew him best, full of laughter and impossible dreams.

Yancy said, "Everybody says the Texians will have to win a war with Mexico first."

"Maybe so, son. Seems General Santa Anna is determined to beat them down. They need all the help they can get."

"Is it true Davy Crockett is going to help them, too?" Tad asked.

"That's what I hear." Pa blew on his coffee to cool it. "The way I see it, freedom is the only thing in this old world worth fighting for. If the Texians go to war with Santa Anna, I mean to be a part of it."

Dismay flickered across Mama's face before her smile slid into place. "If you think that's best, Luther," she said quietly.

"Mama!" Jessie cried. "How can you think of giving up everything, just like that? It's purely scandalous, if you ask me."

"Scandalous?" Pa said. "Jessie girl, how did so many big words get inside one eleven-year-old's head? That's what I want to know."

Then he whirled Mama around the cabin in a wild dance, laughing his reckless laugh that Jessie partly loved and partly didn't.

When at last they stopped, Pa said, "To work! There's plenty to be done if we're to leave tomorrow."

"Tomorrow?" Mama said. "Luther, it's impossible. I've got apples drying, and oh my land, Jessie! I'll bet the wash pot has boiled bone-dry."

"Forget about apples!" Pa said. "Never mind that old wash pot. We've got more important things to do."

"We still have to eat, Pa," Yancy reminded him.

"We'll forage for food," Pa said, spreading his arms wide. "It'll be an adventure!"

Then he began giving orders.

"Jessie, go see about that wash pot. Put the fire out, if it's not out already, and hang the clothes up. They'll be dry by tomorrow morning. Yancy, get those boards out of the toolshed and we'll make some crates. There are plenty of nails in my saddlebags."

"What can I do, Pa?" Tad asked.

"Keep an eye on Callie. Don't let her wander off."

"Taking care of babies is a girl's job!" Tad said. "I'm nigh on to eight years old. Practically growed up. I should be doing a man's work."

Pa's mouth curved into a smile. "I reckon you should at that. Put Callie in her crib, then, and help Yancy with those boards."

Jessie worked far into the night, helping load the wagon with dishes and quilts, coils of rope, buckets and shovels, candles and soap. Then she packed the three things she loved most in all the world. First, the rag doll with china-blue button eyes and yellow yarn hair that

7

Mama made for her last Christmas. Then the shiny red hair ribbons Pa brought her last spring from the general store in Smathers' Bluff. And last, the book of stories she won at school that year for learning more new words than anybody else. Even Yancy.

When morning came, Pa and Yancy saddled their horses. Mama settled herself on the wagon seat with Callie and Jessie. Tad hopped up and Mama flicked the reins. "Bye, Hickory Creek!" he cried. "We're gone to Texas."

Gone to Texas.

2

The TRAVELERS

Pa and Yancy rode their horses in front. Mama followed with the wagon. Sometimes Jessie sat beside Mama, holding Callie on her lap. Sometimes she walked with Tad beside the wagon, fitting her footsteps into the hard brown ruts other wagons had made.

For three days they followed a river. At night they camped along the bank, and Yancy and Pa caught fish for their supper. When it was time to sleep, Mama made their beds inside the wagon. Curled beneath her blankets, Jessie watched the fat, cold moon rising above the trees, its light turning the silent fields to blue. *Eerie,* Jessie decided, was the word that described it best.

On the afternoon of the fourth day, Pa said, "The road ahead looks mighty rough. I'd better drive the wagon." He climbed up beside Mama and smiled at Jessie. "You can take my horse if Yancy will ride along beside you."

9

Yancy adjusted the saddle on his own horse, then handed Diablo's reins to Jessie. "He's got a stubborn streak," he warned. "Don't let him run away with you."

Jessie scratched the reddened insect bites on her arm and fished a dried leaf from her hair. She was bone tired and already sick of beans, beans, and more beans. "I wish Diablo *would* run away with me," she muttered. "I wish he'd take me clear back to Hickory Creek. I'd rather sleep in a cave and eat berries than go to Texas."

Yancy grinned and swung into his saddle. "Complaining won't change things one bit. Are you coming or not?"

Leaving her doll to keep Callie company, Jessie took up Diablo's reins and settled herself into Pa's worn saddle.

They nudged the horses into an easy canter and soon left the wagon far behind. As sunset came, the air cooled, and Jessie shivered inside her dress.

"Jessie?" Yancy's wide green eyes rested on hers. "You look sadder than a caged-up coonhound on Saturday night. Are you all right?"

"I guess so."

"Hey, you think I can't see when something's bothering you?"

"It's not *something*," she blurted, "it's everything!"

"Whoa." Yancy halted his horse and grabbed Diablo's reins. "What's the matter?"

Jessie started to cry. It was as if a whole lifetime of tears suddenly wanted out of her. She leaned into

Diablo's warm neck and sobbed as if her heart would never mend.

Yancy dismounted, then gently lifted her off Diablo. "Let's have it. Whatever it is, it can't be all that bad."

So she told him. How she was mad at Pa for dragging them clear to Texas. How she dreaded having to start over in a new place. How the only thing in the whole world she wanted was one single place to call home.

"I hate being in this family!" she cried. "We live like gypsies! I pretend we're ordinary, but anybody with one eye and half sense can see we're not. Why can't we be like other people?"

Yancy grinned his lopsided grin. "Because we're McCanns. Pa is the most un-ordinary person in all of Kentucky, and good or bad, he's our pa. We're stuck with him."

He wiped her face with his bandanna. "How's that? Better?"

"I suppose." And truly, telling Yancy her troubles did make her feel better. It always had. Yet her problem still lay there, heavy as lead. "But Yancy, whenever people see me in town, I hear them whispering. "There goes that McCann girl. What scheme will that pa of hers think of next?' Why can't Pa ever settle down?"

"I'm not exactly sure," Yancy said. "Seems like Pa is always expecting more out of life than life wants to give back, and he can't stand to be disappointed."

"Doesn't he care how people talk about us?" Jessie asked. "Remember when we went to Riverton to help

11

him unload those turkeys, and those two old women were gossiping about Pa's gambling? I was so embarrassed I wanted to disappear clean off the face of the earth. And Mama was so purely mortified, she wouldn't go to church the next week, for fear people would talk."

"I remember."

"I didn't let them beat me, though," Jessie said. "I told them exactly what I thought of their wagging tongues! Bumptious old crows."

Yancy grinned. "I remember that, too. But Jess, you can't keep blurting out whatever comes into that head of yours. When you go around speaking your mind, and using all those ten-dollar words, it makes people talk. Why, half the time even I don't understand what you're talking about."

"That's not one bit true!" Jessie declared. "You're the smartest boy I ever met. Why, I get the collywobbles just thinking about what would happen if you weren't around to save us from Pa's foolishness."

"Pa's a little strange sometimes, but I'm proud of him for wanting to make a better life for us. Even if he has to fight the Mexicans to do it."

"Will there be a fight, Yancy?"

"Volunteers are pouring in from all over Georgia and Tennessee. If Santa Anna picks a fight, the Texians won't have to face him alone."

"I can just picture Pa now," Jessie said, "standing right smack in the middle of the whole Texian army,

12

throwing out his arms and yelling, 'It'll be an adventure!' "

"It's too soon to worry about it." Yancy shaded his eyes. "Looks like we've got company."

Two men came walking up the dusty trail, their haversacks clanking.

"Mount up," Yancy said quietly. "We'd better go get Pa."

They rode back to the wagon and Yancy reported on the two men.

"Splendid!" Pa said. "I was getting lonely out here myself. It'll be good to have some company. Catch up on the news."

Quickly, Mama wiped Callie's sticky fingers and ran her comb through the baby's yellow curls. Then she poured water over her comb and raked it through Tad's hair. Tad scowled.

"What's the matter, Taddie?" Yancy asked, grinning. "You look like you've just eaten a bowl of cockleburrs."

"Just look at my hair!" Tad cried. "Now it's all wet, for gosh sakes! It's not like we're going to a wedding or a funeral or nothing. It's just two old men, and they probably stink worse than a rotten skunk."

"First impressions are important," Mama said. Her gaze rested on Jessie. "What's wrong with you? Your eyes are all red."

"I'm all right," Jessie said.

"Well, straighten your braids, and wipe the dust off your shoes. Yancy, your shirt is unbuttoned. And stand up straight. You're bowed over like a willow in a hurricane."

Pa chuckled. "Stop fussing, Ruth. I expect these men are used to seeing folks with a bit of dust on them."

Mama squinted into her looking glass. "Mercy, I look a fright."

"No, you don't," Pa said, kissing her cheek. "You're the prettiest woman in the state of Kentucky. Maybe in the whole darn country."

"You're just hoping I'll drive that wagon for you again tomorrow." She smiled at him in the looking glass.

Jessie rolled her eyes. All Pa had to do was say a few sugary words, and Mama acted positively sappy.

Soon the two travelers appeared. They were dressed in rough clothes and weighted down with haversacks and powder horns and hunting knives. Each of them carried a Kentucky rifle.

"How do?" Pa said, sticking out his hand. "McCann's the name. From Hickory Creek, Kentucky."

"Hidy." The man who spoke had side-whiskers, a dirty gray beard, and squinty eyes that made it hard to tell their color. When he took off his battered hat, his bald head shone like a new coin. "Folks call me Curly. Ain't that a hoot?"

Pa laughed, and Curly jerked his thumb at his companion. "This here's Willie. He's ugly as sin, but harmless. He don't talk much."

"We're fixing to have a bite of supper," Pa said. "It ain't much, but you fellows are welcome to join us."

"Much obliged," Curly said, setting down his pack. "We are a mite wore out."

While Mama hurried to add more potatoes to the rabbit stew, Jessie took some leftover biscuits from a tin pail. But Willie preferred his own food and his own dishes. From his haversack, he brought out a hunk of dried venison and a corn pone that banged onto his plate like a rock.

When the meal was ready, Curly tucked into his bowl of stew as if he hadn't eaten in a hundred years. Between bites, he talked to Pa. "Headed for Texas, are you?"

"Sure am. I hear the land is prime and practically free for the asking."

"From what I hear, Old Santy Anna aims to keep Texas for hisself," Curly said. "You may have a harder time claiming that land than you think." His eyes swept over the McCanns. "Specially with a pack of kids along. Are all these yours?"

"They are." Pa introduced them all in turn. "And this beautiful woman is my wife, Ruth."

Curly bobbed his bald head. "Pleased to make your acquaintance, ma'am."

Then he said to Pa, "How are you aiming to get there?"

"We'll take a steamer from Louisville to New Orleans. From there, a schooner to Velasco."

"Velasco," he said, stroking his beard. "I've heard of it. But I don't reckon you'll be farming that land. From what I understand, it's all swamp."

Willie laughed, an unpleasant sound that reminded Jessie of a squeaking wagon wheel. "Haw haw! Maybe you could raise mosquitoes. Or snakes. I bet snakes would grow real good there."

Mama's face paled, but her expression stayed smooth as stone. *Serene,* Jessie thought. Mama shifted Callie onto her other knee. "If Velasco doesn't work out, we'll go somewhere else. Surely all of Texas isn't a swamp."

Jessie's face ached with the effort of keeping her smile pasted on, pretending to be excited. Scrambling to her feet, she ran toward the river. It had all happened so fast, as if a bolt of lightning had hit their cabin and changed everything. One day she was going to school, doing sums, and practicing for the Christmas play. And the next she was on this endless, dusty journey to a place full of mosquitoes and snakes.

"Jess, honey." Mama's footsteps rustled in the dead grass.

"What?"

"I know you're upset. This trip is hard on all of us. But we have to trust Pa to do the right thing."

"Why? He never has before!"

"Jessie Elizabeth McCann!" The look in Mama's eyes was hot enough to fry bacon. "I haven't spanked you since you were three years old. But if you don't start be-

16

having better where your father is concerned, I will whip you within an inch of your life."

Jessie was stunned. Never had she heard Mama sound so cross.

"But Mama . . ."

"Hush for once and listen to me. I know you didn't want to come. Neither did I. Don't you think I worry about it every single minute?"

"Then why didn't you tell Pa no? He wouldn't have come without you." Jessie stared into the darkness.

Settling herself on the grass, Mama wrapped her arms around her knees. "Maybe I should have refused. But all his life your pa's searched for some way to make his mark in the world. Somehow, nothing he's ever tried has worked out the way he planned."

Jessie remembered the failed farms, the turkey experiment, the dusty tinker's shop with its tangle of broken tools.

"When he got it in his head to join with the Texians, I didn't have the heart to stand in his way," Mama said. "Disappointment is like a sickness, Jess. It can bring a person down quick as a fever. Do you understand?"

Jessie wasn't sure just what Mama meant, but said, "I guess so."

"So will you try to be patient with Pa? If not for his sake, for mine."

What choice did she have? It was a long way to Texas. Pa said it would take at least eight days once they

17

reached Louisville. That seemed like a long time to walk around feeling mad. "I'll try."

"Good girl." Mama stood up. "Perhaps the Texians will get what they want without a fight, and Pa will get his farm. That would be good for all of us, wouldn't it?"

Hand in hand, they went back to the fire. Willie was still chewing his venison, leaning against his pack. Curly was showing Tad his rifle. In Yancy's arms, Callie slept soundly, her tiny fingers still curled around a rock she'd found.

Taking out his fiddle, Pa said, "There you are, Jessie. Dance for me. You know the one I mean."

"Oh, Pa."

"Please. Just a short one."

Be patient with Pa, Mama's voice said in her head. So Jessie danced, lifting her arms over her head until her fingers touched. She twirled around in time to the music, bending from the waist, first left and then right, until her long brown braids swept the ground. She could not have said where she learned this dance, or when. She knew only that she had always danced for Pa, and that it seemed to make him happy.

When the music ended, the two travelers clapped. Tad put his fingers to his mouth and whistled. Callie woke and began to cry.

"Here, Mama," Yancy said. "You'd better take her. She fussed nearly the whole time you were gone."

"Time for bed, Tad," Mama said, nuzzling the baby's neck. "You too, Jess. No arguments."

18

The two travelers stood up. "Much obliged for the stew," Curly said. "And for the fine musical entertainment. I hope you find what you're looking for in Texas."

Willie grunted and bobbed his head. Hoisting their packs, they ambled toward the river.

Thunder rumbled in the distance. Pa looked up. "Storm's rolling in. Give me a hand, Yancy."

They unrolled a heavy oilcloth and tied it down with ropes to make a cover for the wagon. Inside, on her bed of blankets, Jessie listened to the rain blowing and the trees tossing in the wind. Despite Mama's explanation, she didn't see how a person could die from disappointment. Every time Pa took a notion to start over somewhere else, forcing her to leave behind all that was dear and familiar, a deep sadness settled over her heart. But she was still alive, still hoping things would turn out differently this time.

When morning came, they set off again, the wagon pitching and groaning along the muddy road. Callie cried and cried and wouldn't stop. Tad whined until Pa grew cross. Worst of all, Yancy rode far ahead of the wagon for most of the day and didn't speak to Jessie at all. It was miserable. *Wretched.*

Then, just as Jessie was certain she wouldn't last one more night in the wilderness, they came at last to Louisville. At the livery, Pa sold the wagon and the oxen and the horses. Jessie cried when Diablo's new owner led him away.

Pa settled them at an inn near the levee. From their window, Jessie could see the boats rocking on the water, and the draymen hauling loads of cargo to the pier.

"You just rest yourself, Ruth," Pa said. "I'll go have a look around."

"Can I look around, too, Pa?" Tad asked. "I ain't never seen a town as big as Louisville."

"Maybe later," Pa said. "Not now." He picked up his hat.

"Go with him, Yancy," Mama said. "You never know what can happen in a town this big."

But Jessie knew what Mama was thinking. Don't let Pa gamble his money away. It had happened before.

In the morning, they boarded the steamer. Jessie watched the sailors roll the heavy wooden barrels down the plank and into the belly of the boat. Soon the whistle blared and the gangplank was raised.

"Up, Jessie!" Callie demanded, standing on her tiptoes. "Let me see."

Jessie picked her up. Callie squealed and waved to the people lining the pier. Clouds of steam puffed out, the whistle sounded again, and the boat began to move.

"Goodbye, Kentuck, hello Texas!" Pa laughed his happy laugh. "You'll like Velasco, Jessie girl. You just wait and see."

"I hope so, Pa." Standing at the rail with Callie in her arms, Jessie watched the town, and her old life, slide away.

3

VELASCO

The steamer's whistle blared as the boat nosed the pier. Standing with Mama and Tad near the front of the boat, Jessie sighed with relief. The trip on the drafty, crowded steamer had taken five days, with stops for wood and water, passengers, and freight along the way.

Their journey to New Orleans had taken them past vast fields of cotton and sugarcane, down a wide, curving river shaded with moss-covered trees. Fish flopped in the tea-colored water, and along the muddy shoreline, strange-looking birds searched for fish. Even the air felt different here. Heavy and damp.

But it was not over yet, Jessie reminded herself. From New Orleans, they would travel to Velasco. Remembering Willie's warning about snakes and mosquitoes, she wished Pa would decide to stay in New Orleans. It was the prettiest town she'd ever seen.

From the steamer's deck, she saw church spires rising above the treetops. Rows of shops and houses lined the shady streets beyond the levee, their iron gates gleaming in the sunlight. Far below, men scurried about the wharves, shouting to each other in strange languages as they loaded and unloaded the steamers. Ladies in fine silk dresses and matching parasols arrived in carriages with servants to carry their trunks to the loading dock. Drays and carts rattled along the streets, steamboats huffed, horses neighed. Cargo nets swung back and forth, like giant black cobwebs against the bright sky. Jessie chose a word to describe it. *Majestic.*

A gleaming paddlewheeler churned its way up the broad brown river and eased to a stop alongside their steamer.

"Pa! Look at that!" Tad crowed, pointing. "The *Nancy B*! Are we going to Texas on her?"

"I'm afraid not, son. We need a smaller boat for traveling on the Brazos River." He pointed to a battered schooner tied up opposite them. "See that boat over there? The one with the green hull?"

"That old bucket?" Tad sounded disappointed. "If we get into a storm, she'll sink like a rock."

Pa laughed. "She's a lot more stable then you think. Bigger, too. Carries fifty people, Captain Baxter says."

Just then a man the McCanns had met on board joined them at the rail and tipped his hat. "Good morning, Mrs. McCann. How's your baby girl today?"

"Much better, Dr. Wilson. I can't thank you enough for your help."

He nodded. "Most babies get sick aboard ship. Motion interferes with their sense of balance and that makes them vomit. Just keep giving her that peppermint oil and she'll be right as rain once you're on dry land again."

"That can't come soon enough for me. I've had enough traveling to last me the rest of my life."

"Velasco's not far," he said kindly. "If this good weather holds, you'll be there in a few days."

"Are you going to live in Velasco too?" Tad asked.

"No, I'm going further inland, to San Antonio. The garrison there needs a doctor. I figure that's the best way I can help the Texians win their freedom."

Yancy, who had been listening quietly, said to Dr. Wilson, "Will there really be a fight with Mexico?"

"I don't see how it can be avoided. The Mexicans have gone back on their promises once too often. Stephen Austin tried his best to reason with them, but all he got for his trouble was a year and a half in jail."

"They're a stubborn lot," Pa said. "But so are we Kentuckians. Santa Anna's liable to get more than he bargained for."

The steamer's whistle blasted again. "Time to go ashore," Pa said.

He took Callie from Mama's arms and they all went down the gangplank and onto the sunny pier. Jessie felt dizzy. Her legs wobbled. Dr. Wilson smiled down at her.

"Takes a moment to get your land legs back. You'll be fine in no time."

He said to Pa, "I'm off to visit a friend till the boat sails for Velasco. I'll see you on board."

Pa left them there while he went to arrange for their belongings to be loaded onto the schooner. Then he came back with a greasy brown paper that smelled of sugar and cinnamon.

"Hot pastries!" he announced, handing them around. "A New Orleans specialty."

"Mmm." Tad licked his lips. "When we get to Velasco, I want this for breakfast every single day."

"You won't be getting anything this fancy," Pa said. "Not for a while at least." His eyes sought Mama's. "It seems some of what we've heard of Velasco may be true. It won't be anything like New Orleans."

"I didn't expect it would be," Mama said, her gaze steady. "Whatever is there, we'll make the best of it."

"If it turns out to be too bad, I'll send you and the children back to Kentucky," Pa said. "You can stay with your aunt Lucille, till I'm established. Then when the war is over, and the farm is up and running, you can come back."

"Certainly not," Mama said. "I didn't come all this way only to turn around and go back again. Besides, travel costs money. We need all our cash to buy the land you want."

Pa rested his hand on her hair. "You're a remarkable woman, Ruth McCann."

"Stubborn, you mean," Yancy said, grinning. "Stubborn as a Kentucky mule."

"Families are meant to be together," Mama declared. "I wouldn't sleep a wink if we were back there and your pa was down here by himself. We'll stick it out. No matter how bad it is. I'll have no more talk about it. Luther, find us some water. We're thirsty and sticky."

Pa came back with water, and they all drank. With Mama's dampened handkerchief, they wiped their faces and fingers. Soon it was time to board the schooner for Velasco.

The schooner was even more uncomfortable than the steamer. There were no real cabins, just hard benches below the decks where the light was murky and the air heavy with the stench of sweat and grease. Crowded in with the other passengers, Jessie felt her stomach heave as the anchor was lifted and the boat swayed on the river. From the bench across from her, Pa smiled and winked.

Jessie scowled.

"You'd better be careful, or your face will freeze that way," Yancy teased. "Then what will you do?" He tipped her face up to his. "What's the matter now?"

"Just look at Pa. Grinning like he's in some fine music hall, instead of stuffed into this revolting old boat like a human sausage."

"He's happy, all right," Yancy said. "Mama's trying hard not to spoil it for him. We should too."

"Well, I am tired of it," Jessie grumbled. "I can't wait

till I'm grown up. Pa won't tell me what to do then. He won't drag me around anymore, either."

She closed her eyes and when she opened them again, Dr. Wilson was standing over her with a small glass bottle and a cloth that smelled of peppermint. "Here," he said kindly. "Breathe through this. It'll make you feel better."

"If you want to make me feel better, make my bull-headed pa put down some roots somewhere. Preferably in the United States of America."

"Pardon?"

"Don't mind her," Yancy said. "She's in one of her Kentucky tempers. Say thank you to the doctor, Jess."

"Thank you," Jessie mumbled. She took a deep breath into the cloth. It made her feel better.

Later, when her legs felt cramped and knotted as the ship's ropes, Yancy took her topside. It was nighttime on the river. The moon made ripples of light on the black water. Behind them, the wake swirled and foamed. The wind sang in the sails, pushing them through the water like an arrow in the dark.

"How can the captain see to steer?" she asked.

"He doesn't need to see," Yancy said. "He's sailed these waters so often he could do it blindfolded. He knows every sandbar and shoal between New Orleans and Velasco."

The wind whipped her hair and Jessie tucked it behind her ears. "Yancy, will Velasco be as awful as everyone says?"

26

"Beats me. But Pa sure is excited. He says we can buy four thousand acres of prime land for a hundred and twenty dollars, and we don't even have to pay for it all at once. We'll pay a little bit each year." He paused, thinking. "You know how much four thousand acres would cost back home? Thousands. And nobody would wait for their money, either."

Jessie shrugged. Yancy tugged her braids. "Try not to get too excited, Jess. My heart can't take the strain."

He was joking, but Jessie didn't see anything funny. "It won't matter if we get ten thousand acres or ten million. Pa won't stay put very long."

The old schooner shuddered as it changed direction. Bracing herself against the rail, Jessie said, "I can't tell which Pa wants more. The land, or the chance to fight."

"I know. When he talks about it, he gets a strange look in his eyes, as if he's got a fever inside him." Yancy held out his hand. "Come on. Let's get some sleep."

Down below, some of the men had cleared a space on the deck and were playing cards with Pa and Dr. Wilson.

"Well, that's it for me," the doctor said, tossing aside his cards. "I'm afraid I'm not much of a gambler."

Pa stood up, rattling coins in his hands. "I'd better quit, too, before I hit a losing streak."

"Before Mama finds out, he means," Yancy muttered. "Don't tell her, all right, Jess? She's already worried about Callie."

27

"I won't tell!" Jessie said. "I know when to keep quiet."

"I reckon you do at that." Yancy put his arm around her. "You've got a level head on your shoulders. No matter what happens when we get to Texas, you'll be all right."

The next morning, when Jessie went on deck again, it was as if she'd sailed into yet another world. The schooner slid through the brown water, past low swampy lands thick with reeds. Standing at the rail with some of the other passengers, Jessie watched a flock of long-beaked birds poking in the ropy grasses along the shore.

"Those are herons," Dr. Wilson explained. "And look over there, Jessie. Alligators!"

Two scaly gray creatures slithered along the swamplands. One slid into the water, sending a pool of bubbles to the surface.

"They look like logs with eyes!" Jessie said. Just then, the other one opened its enormous mouth, showing rows of needlelike teeth. "Ferocious logs," she added.

"You wouldn't want to get crosswise with one," Dr. Wilson agreed. "One time when I was hunting in Louisiana, I saw an alligator bring down a fawn, quick as a wink."

Soon they sailed into deeper water, at a place the sailors called the southwest pass. The wind came up and the old schooner rolled and tossed like a twig in the angry waters. Everyone got sick. Too sick to move or talk. The whole boat smelled of vomit and sweat. Mama lay beside Callie below decks. Tad leaned against Pa for hours at a time, his little face white and pinched. Yancy and Jessie stayed on deck. It was crowded, but at least the air was cleaner. Everyone seemed to take turns vomiting into the churning waters. Jessie's head throbbed. Her tongue felt thick and furry. She was dazed with hunger, but too sick to eat.

For three days the schooner rolled and bucked in the storm. Finally, they crossed the bar and anchored at the mouth of the river.

The bedraggled passengers staggered ashore. Two men were met by a woman wearing buckskin trousers and a felt hat. They hauled themselves and their belongings onto her wagon. Soon it disappeared down the dusty road. Another man wobbled into a gray wooden building with the word *Saloon* painted on the side.

"Is this Velasco?" Tad asked weakly. "Are we home?"

"This is it." Pa led them to the porch of a general store. "Wait here. Yancy and I will get our things."

Wearily, Mama sank onto a wooden bench. "Thank God we're finally here."

Only someone as religious as Mama could be thankful for Velasco. It was little more than a village, no bigger than Smathers' Bluff. Jessie counted another store, six saloons, and a weather-beaten hotel with a sign that read *Closed for Winter*. Beyond the pier and the cluster of crude buildings, the land stretched toward the horizon, low, brown, and flat as a plate.

Jessie wanted to cry. A fat black bug scurried across her shoe and burrowed into the dust. She slapped at something big and green that landed on her arm and stung her, right through her dress.

29

"Jessie, what's the matter with you?" Mama asked.

"The bugs! They're eating me alive. Can't you feel them?"

Mama slapped at one on her neck. "Surely there's some way to keep them away."

"Not likely, ma'am."

A boy about Yancy's age, with red hair and freckles, grinned at them. "Howdy, folks. Welcome to Velasco."

"Thank you." Mama brushed a bug off Callie's pinched little face.

"My name's James Talbot. This here's my ma's store. And I'm sorry to say, we don't have any remedy for the skeeters. After a while you'll get to where you won't hardly even notice 'em."

"I doubt that." Mama smiled at him. "Have you anything to drink in that store of yours? Anything at all for colic? My baby has been sick for days."

"Southwest pass is a real bear when a norther kicks up. I'm not sure about medicine, ma'am, but I think there's some lemonade, or my ma can make tea."

Inside the store, the wood-scented air was warm and still. Flies buzzed about a jar of lemon drops on the counter.

"Can I have a lemon drop, Mama?" Tad asked.

"Tad."

"Oh, let him have one," said the woman behind the counter, shooing the flies away. "Poor little thing looks famished. It's on the house."

"What do you say, Tad?" Mama prompted.

"Thanks." Tad popped the candy into his mouth.

"You're welcome." The woman smiled at Mama. "I'm Mary Talbot."

"Ruth McCann. These are my children, Jessie, Tad, and Callie. My older son, Yancy, is helping his father. Would you have anything for colic? The baby's sick."

"I'm sorry, I don't have a thing except some milk and mustard plaster. Maybe she'll feel better after a decent night's sleep. Where you folks from?"

"Kentucky."

"Long trip," Mrs. Talbot observed. "Well, welcome to Texas."

Pa and Yancy came in. Right away, Jessie could tell there was something wrong. The corners of Pa's mouth turned down, and he stared at the floor, as if he couldn't bear to look them in the eye.

"What is it?" Mama asked.

Yancy said, "Remember what that Curly fellow said about Velasco? Well, it's all true. There's nothing here but this store and something called a resort, and some saloons."

"Saloons?" Tad's eyes went wide. "With real pianos and real dancing girls? Can I go see?"

"Hush, Tad," Mama said. "Luther, what about the land upriver?"

Pa shook his head. "Too dry to fish and too wet to plow."

31

"There's another town across the river," Yancy said. "It's called Quintana. The man at the boat dock said . . ."

"You don't want to go to Quintana," Mrs. Talbot put in. "Nothing there but shanties and a bunch of rowdy army recruits. It's no place to raise a family."

"Well, Pa, what now?" Jessie asked, her voice tight with anger.

Before he could answer, two sailors from the schooner pushed their way into the store. The taller one said, "Mr. McCann, we got all your things unloaded. Will you be needing to rent a wagon?"

Pa studied them for a moment. Then he said, "I don't want to rent one. I want to buy one. And a good team of oxen, too."

Tad's mouth dropped open and his candy plopped onto the floor. "Are we going back to Kentucky, Pa?"

"No, we're going to a place called San Antonio de Béxar. I've spoken with Dr. Wilson about it, and I'm convinced it's the best thing to do."

"San Antonio?" Mrs. Talbot brightened. "That's more like it."

"You've been there?" Mama asked, a note of hope creeping into her voice.

"No, but my husband made several trips there before he died. It's a real town, Mrs. McCann. More than twelve hundred people, the last I heard. There's a school for the children, at least part of the time, and an excellent general store. My Frank used to talk about all the peddlers who stopped off there."

Pa was grinning now, as if going to San Antonio de Béxar had been his plan all along. "It's settled then. I'm going right now to find a team and a wagon, and we'll leave first thing tomorrow. It'll be an adventure!"

Mrs. Talbot put an arm around Mama's shoulders. "Don't worry. There's a garrison at San Antonio de Béxar, too. It's probably the safest place in all of Texas at the moment. Now, the hotel is closed for the season, but you're welcome to stay here tonight."

"Thank you. We're much obliged."

"Glad to have you. I don't get too many visitors this time of year. It'll be a pleasure to have some female company."

Mrs. Talbot showed them to a room behind the store. There was a fireplace, two chairs, and a table with an oil lamp. Then she cooked a supper of fish and rice and corn.

Mama spooned some rice into Callie's mouth, but Callie made an awful face and spit it out. "No, Mama!"

"Poor little thing," Mrs. Talbot said. "She's all tuckered out."

"I hope that's all it is," Mama said, but she didn't sound convinced.

Later, Mrs. Talbot brought quilts and blankets and made beds on the floor. It was warm in the little room. The murmur of the women's voices and the patter of rain on the roof lulled Jessie to sleep. When morning came the McCanns said goodbye to the Talbots, loaded everything onto the wagon Pa bought, and set off for San Antonio.

4

ANGELINA

Day after day the wagon rolled across a hilly, broken land thick with fat, thorny trees and tangled vines. To Jessie it seemed that every day there was another river to cross; one day the rushing rust-red Colorado, the next the gentle Navedad, and after that the calm, blue Guadelupe, until, at last, they reached the road to San Antonio de Béxar.

Late one afternoon, they crested a hill. Pa stopped the wagon and pointed to a church bell tower rising above the thicket of distant trees. Just ahead lay San Antonio at last and all his golden dreams.

"See, Ruth?" he said. "Just like I promised. We're almost there."

Peering over Pa's shoulder, Jessie shaded her eyes against the white glare. The empty landscape seemed to go on forever. *Desolate* was the word that came into her mind, but she didn't say it out loud.

"Please hurry, Luther," Mama cried. "Callie's getting worse. I simply don't know what to do for her. Please."

"Dr. Wilson will know what to do," Yancy said. "He'll make Callie well in no time. Don't worry, Mama."

"We won't see Dr. Wilson for a while." Pa flicked the reins hard and the wagon trundled on. "He's heading for Gonzales."

"Isn't he going to be the doctor for the garrison here?" Yancy asked.

"He is. But he's going to Gonzales first, to convince the Mexican loyalists they should come over to our side."

Mama frowned. "What am I going to do about this sick child? What?"

"We'll find someone," Pa soothed. "Maybe there's another doctor in town. Surely someone there knows how to cure a simple stomachache."

Mama's voice was sharp. "If it were only a simple stomachache, Luther, I could cure her myself. Just look at her! She needs a doctor! *Now!*"

Jessie kissed Callie's hot little neck. "Hey, Callie-wallie," she crooned. "Want to play with my doll? Want to play this little piggy?"

Callie blinked and turned her head away. One fat tear slid down her face.

"Hey, Callie," Tad said. "Don't cry. Watch this."

With two fingers he pulled out his cheeks, then crossed his eyes and wiggled his tongue. "I'm a scary monster, and I'm coming to get you! *Boo!*"

Callie's blue eyes widened. Then she screamed.

Mama whirled around. "Tad! Stop torturing her! Can't you see how sick she is?"

"I'm sorry, Mama. I was only trying to help."

"You can help by being quiet till we get to town. Not another word. And keep your feet still!"

It was nearly dark when the wagon tore across a log bridge above yet another river and then into narrow, twisting streets that glowed softly in the torchlight. Through open doorways came the sounds of a strange, musical language and strumming guitars. Spicy smells scented the air.

They hurtled past a plaza bustling with people and horses and oxcarts, and pulled up short at an inn. Pa snatched Callie out of Jessie's arms and ran in.

Jessie called out, "She'll be all right, won't she, Mama?"

But Mama didn't answer her. "Yancy, take care of the children," she said, her voice tight. "I'll be out as soon as I can. Don't move."

Too tired and too worried to ask again, Jessie waited in the wagon with her brothers, listening to the music and the lovely, lilting language. She closed her eyes and made a wish. All she wanted was a doctor for her little sister. Then maybe a dinner without a single bean in it, and a soft featherbed all to herself.

Tad spoke first. "Is that the Mexicans singing?" he whispered.

"I reckon," Yancy said. "It's pretty, ain't it?"

"What do you think they're saying?" Tad asked.

"It's a song about love," said someone from the darkness.

"Who's there?" Yancy called out.

A girl stepped from the shadows. In the flickering torchlight, Jessie saw only a slender shape, dark, wide-set eyes, and a tumble of shiny black curls.

"My name is Angelina," the girl said. Her soft accent made it sound like a song.

"Angelina," Jessie repeated.

"You must be new here," she said. "I know almost everyone in Béxar, and I have never seen you before."

"We came all the way from Kentuck," Tad said. "We rode a steamship and a schooner. My pa's gonna help Davy Crockett fight the Mex—"

Jessie poked him. "Hush!"

Yancy said, "We need a doctor right quick. Do you know where we can—"

At that moment, Pa yelled from the porch, "Jessie! Boys! Come quick." His voice sounded high and strange. Jessie's stomach coiled.

They scrambled from the wagon and hurried inside. The inn seemed strangely quiet after the bustle of the street. Mama was in the parlor, kneeling. Jessie's heart lurched. No one said anything.

Finally Mama looked up at them. "Callie's gone." She covered her face.

The air stopped moving. Pa just stood there, his hands dangling at his sides. Jessie knelt beside Mama,

37

hot tears scalding her face. Yancy wept silently, tears running down his face. Tad shouted, "No, she isn't! Dr. Wilson will make her all better! He did it before." A woman in a brown dress took him in her arms. Someone else brought a pitcher of cold water.

"Missus," said the woman in the brown dress. "If you need a place to lay out your little girl, you're welcome to stay here. My back room ain't much to look at, but it's quiet and clean."

Mama was too broken to speak. Jessie waited for Pa to say something, but he only stared, a look of utter despair on his tired face. Finally, Yancy wiped his face on his sleeve. "We'd be much obliged." He lifted Callie and began to follow the innkeeper down the hallway. Tad slumped in the corner, his face turned to the wall.

"Jessie," Yancy said calmly, "find a bucket and bring some more water. Tad, go unhitch the team. We won't be going anywhere tonight."

In the small courtyard behind the inn stood a stone well. Jessie filled a bucket and brought it back to the room where Callie lay. Mama began washing Callie, crooning to her as if Callie somehow could still hear her voice.

Jessie could feel her heart breaking up inside her chest. Callie was dead. Callie was dead. She ran outside, to where the wagon waited in the shadows. Pressed against the cold, hard wheel, she cried for Callie, for Pa, for all of them.

A hand touched her shoulder.

"Who's there?"

"It's Angelina. Why are you crying?"

"My little sister." Jessie's breath hitched in her chest. "She was sick forever and now she's dead."

"Oh! *Pobrecita*," Angelina whispered. "No wonder you're so sad."

Dropping to her knees beside the wagon, she steepled her hands, closed her eyes, and began to pray. Jessie couldn't understand the words, but the sound of them, so soft and quiet, soothed her shattered heart.

After Angelina finished her prayer, she waited until Jessie's tears slowed. Then she said, "You have not told me your name."

"Jessie McCann."

"Jessie? That's a boy's name, yes? I have never heard of a girl named Jessie."

"When I grow up, I'm changing it," Jessie said.

"Can you do that?"

"When you're grown up, you can do anything you want."

"Are you sure about this?" Angelina asked.

Jessie nodded. "When I grow up, I'm going to live in one place for the rest of my life and be perfectly ordinary."

"Not me," said Angelina. "I am a woman of great ambition. I want to be famous and rich and ride with the *vaqueros*."

"Will you stay here?"

"I don't know. I suppose so."

The sound of Pa's boots on the porch broke into the darkness. "Jessie! Come inside now. Your mama's asking for you."

Jessie turned away. "I must go."

Angelina unfastened something at her neck and pressed it into Jessie's hand. "Tomorrow afternoon," she whispered. "Late. Meet me under the river bridge." She pointed. "It's just there, beyond those trees at the end of the road."

"But . . . ," Jessie began.

"Go on now. Your papa is waiting."

"Jessie?" Pa called again.

Jessie went up the steps to the inn. Pa wrapped his arms around her, hugging her so tightly she thought her ribs would break. She could feel his breath on her hair, could feel grief pouring out of him. Together they crossed the porch and went to the room where Callie lay. For the rest of the night they sat there, not talking, just holding on to each other.

When morning came, Jessie stood up. Something dropped to the floor with a bright tinkling sound. Pa picked it up. "What's this?"

A small silver star hung from a matching chain. It glittered in the watery light coming through the window. "It's mine," Jessie said, reaching for it. "Angelina gave it to me."

"Angelina?" Pa asked.

"She came to our wagon last night," Tad explained. "While we were waiting for you and Mama."

"Angelina," Pa said again. "Sounds Mexican to me." He looked down at Jessie. "You're to have nothing to do with Mexicans. Nothing."

"Please, Pa. Let me keep it."

"No, Jessie." Pa's eyes were like two black stones. "I mean it."

"Luther," Mama said wearily. "Let her keep it. What harm can it do?"

"What harm can it do? Mexicans are not like us, Ruth. They can't be trusted." He turned the necklace over in his palm. "Next week, that girl could have the law after you, Jessie, claiming you stole this."

"She wouldn't do that," Jessie said. "It's not . . . logical."

"They're not logical. That girl might send somebody to shoot you, for all I know." He pointed his finger at her. "You stay away from her, you hear me?"

Anger and grief piled up against Jessie's heart till she thought it would burst. "I hate you!" she yelled. "Why couldn't *you* have died instead of Callie? We'd all be better off!"

"Jessie McCann!" Mama shot to her feet. "You take that back. Apologize to Pa this instant!"

"I won't!" Jessie stamped her foot. "If he hadn't brought us to this horrible place, Callie wouldn't be dead. But she *is* dead! Because of him and his stupid schemes! He never changes!"

Without warning, Mama slapped her hard. Jessie drew back, stunned, trembling with anger.

"Mama!" Yancy pulled Jessie into his arms. "Don't

cry," he whispered into her ear. "She didn't mean it. And Pa will change his mind. He always does."

"I shouldn't have hit you, Jess," Mama said tiredly. "I'm sorry for that. But you can't be disrespectful to your pa. Tell him you're sorry for what you said."

Jessie didn't feel sorry. She felt sad and furious. Hiding her hands inside her pockets, she crossed her fingers so her words really wouldn't count. "Sorry."

"All right." Pa turned to Mama. "We'll find some-place for Callie's grave, and then we'll rest. We're all too tired to think straight."

Later that day, Pa dug a grave on a shady hillside. After Mama wrapped Callie in her best shawl and laid her in-side the wooden coffin Yancy had gotten from the fu-neral parlor. Jessie set her blue-eyed doll beside her. Then Mama read some Bible verses, and it was over.

They rode back to the inn in silence, and Pa left them there while he looked for a place to live. The brick-red sun was low in the sky when he brought them to a cabin close by the side of the road. When the wagon was finally unloaded and they'd eaten the ash cakes Mama made, Jessie picked up her shawl.

"May I go exploring, Mama?"

"I suppose so. But don't go far, Jess. And be back be-fore dark."

Jessie hurried out before Mama could change her mind. She hardly noticed the cold wind whipping through the streets as she ran toward the bridge, and Angelina.

5

The TEXIAN

Beneath the bridge a small fire burned, casting its yellow glow over the swift-moving water. Arms akimbo, one hip cocked, Angelina watched Jessie pick her way along the slippery bank.

"So," she said, her black eyes full of light, "there you are, Jessie McCann. I was beginning to think you wouldn't come. What a sad day." Her silver bracelets jingling, she reached inside her pocket. "I brought you something from my mama's kitchen. *Sopaipillas.*"

Soapy pillows? Jessie wondered, as the sweet confection, still slightly warm and sticky with honey, melted on her tongue. Why such a peculiar name? There was nothing peculiar about the taste, though. She licked her fingers and smiled. "Ambrosial!"

"I've never heard such a word," Angelina said.

"I love words," Jessie said. "*Ambrosial* means dee-licious!"

Angelina laughed. "My mama is the best cook in San Antonio. Visit us someday and she will make a feast for you."

Jessie nodded, but she knew it would never happen, unless Pa changed his mind.

"You're unhappy again," Angelina said. "Sit here by the fire. I will tell you a story to cheer you up.

"Long ago," she began, "there was a girl called Maria. She lived in a tiny village not far from Mexico City. One day, despite her mama's warnings, she strayed too far from home and was captured by an evil troll." Angelina winked at Jessie. "He lived beneath a bridge, exactly like this one."

Jessie smiled.

"Anyway," she went on, "this evil troll put poor Maria into a sack. Then he went to the city, gathered a crowd, and announced that the sack was magic. With his walking stick, he poked the sack and called out in a loud voice, '¡Canta, Saquito! Sing, little sack!'

"Well, as you can imagine, Maria was too scared not to obey. So she sang the lullaby her mama sang to her every night at bedtime. As it happened, her mama was there, and as soon as she heard the singing, she knew it was Maria inside the sack. So what do you think she did then, Jessie?"

"Chopped off the troll's head!" Jessie cried.

"No!" Angelina whooped. "She said to the troll, 'Take this pot and fetch me some water and I will make you a feast fit for a king.' Of course, as soon as the troll dropped the sack, Maria's mama cut it open and rescued poor, frightened Maria. And so—"

"Shhh!" Jessie grabbed Angelina's arm. "Somebody's coming."

The two girls huddled beside the fire. There was a scraping sound and then Yancy's anxious face appeared. "Jessie?" He leaned against the pillar, waiting for them. "You're Angelina," he said, when they stood face to face. "I'm Jessie's brother, Yancy. I've been looking all over for her."

Tilting her head, Angelina studied him. "You remind me of my brother Antonio. You're not *quite* as handsome as he was, but almost."

When Yancy's face reddened, Angelina laughed. "It's a compliment."

"You're a mite too young to be paying compliments to boys," Yancy said. "You should be home, playing with dolls."

Angelina tossed her curls. "Brothers," she said, "are impossible."

Jessie was too worried to reply. If Pa found out she'd disobeyed him, he'd thrash her for sure.

"Let's go, Jess," Yancy said. "It's getting dark. Mama will worry if we're not back soon." To Angelina he said, "Don't burn the bridge down."

When he turned away, Angelina caught Jessie's arm and whispered, "Tomorrow."

Jessie walked fast to keep up with Yancy's long

strides. As they neared the cabin, she asked, "Are you going to tell Pa?"

He stopped. "Our life is too full of misery already. Why add to it? From now on you'll have to be careful, though. Pay attention to the time. Don't give Pa a reason to come looking for you."

Jessie's heart swelled with happiness. "I love you, Yancy!" she cried.

He laughed. "Come on. We're late."

When they got home, a fire was burning in the grate. Tad was already asleep on his pile of blankets. The crates were unpacked; the clock stood on the mantel next to Mama's china teapot. In the corner stood Pa's fiddle and Mama's spinning wheel. The rag rug Jessie had helped Mama make last winter had been rolled out over the wood floor.

"There you are," Mama said. "Time for bed, Jess."

Pa came in with more wood for the fire. He smiled at Jessie, but his eyes were devoid of light, his grief covering him like a heavy cloak.

Drawing her covers tightly around her shoulders, Jessie said, "Night, Pa."

"Night, Jessie girl."

A few minutes later, he snuffed the candles and Jessie fell asleep.

"Hurry up, Jessie," Mama urged. "Finish peeling those potatoes. Yancy, make yourself useful. Your pa will be here with our guest any minute."

Yancy winked at Jessie. "Don't work yourself into such a dither, Mama. Pa says it's quite a ways out to Mr. Atterbury's place. There's no way they'll be here before five o'clock."

"Exactly. It's nearly four now and there's still so much to do. Where's Tad?"

"Went to put some flowers on Callie's grave," Yancy said quietly. For a moment, they stood still, like people in a painting. It was February now, three months since Callie died, but Jessie had lost track of time. Too many confusing things had happened. Back in November, Stephen Austin left the Texian army to ask the United States for guns and money to help fight Santa Anna. Some men were having meetings to talk about Texian independence. Jessie heard people arguing about it in town. Some said the Mexican constitution was enough, but others wanted an independent nation.

Then, just before Christmas, General Cós brought the Mexican army to San Antonio. A man named Ben Milam came to ask Pa to help him fight. Many people packed up their wagons and fled San Antonio right then, but not the McCanns. They had no place to go. For five days, Jessie hid inside the cabin, listening to the sounds of fighting in the streets. One day Pa came home with sad news. Mr. Milam had been killed in the fighting. But General Cós was defeated. He took his army back across the Rio Grande and promised never to come back. Jessie hoped he would keep his promise, because up till now nothing but bad things had happened since the McCanns came to Texas.

After they had buried Callie, Pa told Jessie that it wouldn't hurt so much in time, that after a while she would feel better. She didn't believe him. Happy things seemed to be over quick as lightning. But bad things stuck like cockleburrs and would never go away.

At first Jessie cried all the time. Everywhere she looked, reminders of Callie made her chest tighten and her eyes go blurry. But now, the hurt was slowly fading, like a summer storm over the mountains. Still, if it weren't for Angelina, Jessie couldn't bear to stay in this place. It reminded her of that awful night, and the terrible things she'd said to Pa. He had forgiven her. She knew that. Forgiving herself was much harder.

Sneaking away to see Angelina was wrong, but it wouldn't last long. In March, when Mr. Edwards returned, school would open again and she wouldn't have time for secrets shared beneath a bridge.

"Jessie, the potatoes?" her mother called.

Tad burst through the door, his eyes shining. "Mama! Look what I found!" He held up a tiny kitten.

"Oh, what a sweet little thing!" Mama reached for the kitten. "It's a girl! Where did you find her, son?"

"By Callie's grave. I was looking for flowers, but there's nothing blooming now. I heard a noise and there she was. Isn't she something?"

"Yes, she is," Mama said. "I'll bet she's hungry. Jessie,

warm some milk and get that blue bowl from the cupboard. The one with the chip in it."

"Oh boy!" Tad crowed. "We're keeping her."

"Just a minute, Tad," Mama said. "You'll have to ask Pa first."

"He won't care. What should we name her?"

"I don't know," Mama said. "What do you think, Jess?"

"Star," Jessie said, because the kitten, so small and perfectly made, reminded her of Angelina's pretty necklace. "I think we should name her Star."

"Come here, Star," Tad crooned, taking the kitten from Mama's arms. "You're going to live with us now."

Mama put her hand on Tad's shoulder. "Our company will be here soon. Go change your shirt. And comb your hair, Tad. You look like a shipwrecked sailor."

Jessie poured milk into the bowl and set it on the floor. The kitten licked greedily until the bowl was shiny.

While Mama mixed corn bread, Jessie and Yancy set the table, putting out Mama's best dishes and the big brown platter for the meat.

At last, Pa opened the door and called, "Ruth! We're here." In he came with Mr. Atterbury.

"Hey, Pa!" Tad cried, holding up the kitten. "Look what I found. Her name is Star. Can I keep her?"

"Star, is it? Well, seeing as how she already has a

49

name and all, I reckon so. But she's your responsibility, Tad. Don't trouble your mama with her."

Everyone said hello and pleased-to-meet-you and won't-you-sit-down, and soon they were all sitting around the table. Pa carved the meat and Mama passed bowls of mashed potatoes and gravy and the corn bread. For dessert, there was bread pudding with raisins, and coffee for the grownups.

While they ate, Pa and Mr. Atterbury talked about the bright future all Texians would have once they were free from Mexico.

"I'm sure you've already found out," Mr. Atterbury said, "that it takes a strong back and a strong will to start over in a brand-new country. But once we're free from Santa Anna, there's a better life waiting for all of us. I've been lots of places, and I can tell you, there's not anywhere else on this earth as beautiful or as full of promise as Texas. Specially for young men like us."

Pa's eyes shone. "That was a fine piece of land you showed me today," he said. "I hope folks won't mind it being settled by a humble tinker from Kentuck."

"We don't mind," Mr. Atterbury said. "Just look around town. All kinds of people on the streets. Doctors, storekeepers, lawyers, pirates. The best thing about Texas, other than its being the most beautiful place the good Lord ever created, is that it don't matter who you are, or what you did in the past. Texians are the kind of folks who welcome new people and new ideas. When you get ready to claim that land, we'll ride over to San Felipe

50

and do it up proper. You might want to wait, though, till this mess with Santa Anna is sorted out."

"It may happen sooner than we think," Pa said. "I heard some talk in town today. They say he's gathered his army just south of the river. They say he's planning an attack."

Mama sent Pa a worried look. "He means to attack here? In San Antonio?"

"Not likely, Miz McCann," Mr. Atterbury said. "But if it looks like Santa Anna is heading this a-way, you just make for the Alamo. You'll be safe there until the fighting stops."

"The Alamo?" Jessie put in. "That old mission? Why, it's . . . dilapidated! It doesn't even have a roof."

"But the walls are four feet thick!" the Texian said. "You just hunker down in there and you'll be all right."

"Thank you," Mama said. "But my husband will know what to do if trouble comes."

Pa's expression changed from uncertainty to excitement. "Ruth," he began. "When we left Kentucky, I told you I intended to help these people get their independence. And it looks like it's time for me to make good on that promise."

"What do you mean?"

"Mr. Atterbury is on his way to Goliad to join up with Colonel Fannin," Pa explained. "Dr. Wilson has decided to go with them, and I intend to go, too."

"You can't leave us here when the entire Mexican army is sitting just across the river."

"Rest easy, ma'am," Mr. Atterbury said. "Santa Anna won't cross the river in the dead of winter. Too hard on the men and the horses. I figure he'll wait it out and make his move come spring. In the meantime, Colonel Fannin needs all the good men he can find."

Yancy turned his spoon around and around on the table, watching it catch the candlelight. "If Pa goes, I'm going, too."

"You're still a boy," Mama said. "Not even sixteen yet. No. I won't hear of it."

Mr. Atterbury smiled. "I know just how you feel, ma'am. But a boy's got to prove himself a man, sooner or later. My own pa fought in the War of 1812 when he was scarcely seventeen."

"Nevertheless." Mama stood up and began clearing the table. The dishes rattled in her hands. "I've already buried one child in this place. That's all I can bear to sacrifice, no matter how glorious the cause."

"I'll be with Pa," Yancy said. "We can look out for each other. Please, Ma. This is something I want to do."

"Why?" Mama turned her back and scraped their plates. "So you can brag to that girl back home about what a brave soldier you were?"

"No," Yancy said quietly. "So Callie's death will mean something. We came here for a better life. When Pa gets that four thousand acres, we'll have a chance to build a home here."

Mama turned around. "I wish you wouldn't, Yancy. Your father's a grown man. This is a choice he makes freely. But you're still so young. You don't realize what you're getting into."

Tad said, "If Yancy goes, *I'm* going."

The plate in Mama's hand crashed to the floor. "Go to bed, Tad! No. Do not speak to me. Just leave the table now. And take that cat with you." She turned to Pa. "See what you've done? You've poisoned all of them with this madness. And for what? Oh, I wish we'd never left home!"

Pa took Mama in his arms. "Don't cry. Nothing will happen to Yancy and me. I promise."

Mr. Atterbury stood up. "Thank you for a fine meal, Miz McCann. Try not to worry. Maybe we can still reason with the Mexicans. They seem to have such a love of freedom themselves. Surely somebody can make them understand why we want it too."

He shook Pa's hand. "We'll leave at first light on Thursday. See Frankie Massey over at the store. He knows what-all you and your boy will need. Old Jonas down at the livery will supply your horses."

Pa and Mama saw the Texian to the door. When he had gone, Mama put water on to boil. Jessie put the tablecloth away. After the dishes were washed and dried, Yancy said, "Walk with me, Jessie."

They went outside. "Are you still meeting Angelina at the bridge?" he asked.

"Almost every day," Jessie said. "I hate keeping it from Pa, but she's a good friend, Yancy. And *her* family has lived here for years and years. Her uncle Julio has a ranch

53

near a town called Liberty. It's been in her family forever. Why, they're more Texian than we'll ever be. She told me we could ride with the *vaqueros* there someday. We've been making plans. You'd like that, wouldn't you?"

"Maybe so," Yancy said. "But don't let Pa hear you say that."

Grabbing a stick, Jessie traced a map. "See, here is Liberty, and here's the ranch—"

Yancy said, "Look, I want you to promise to look after Mama while I'm gone. She acts stronger than she really is. Leaving home and losing Callie was nearly more than she could take."

"Then why are you leaving too? We depend on you. You know that."

"Yes. Now listen hard, Jess. 'Cause this is kinda hard to understand. It's partly Pa. And it's partly because everyone depends on me so much that I decided to go. Sometimes it weighs me down."

"You don't care what happens to us!" Jessie cried. "You don't care if Santa Anna kills us. You're just like Pa, running off on some wild adventure."

"Now you're being plain dumb," Yancy said. "You *know* how Pa is. He acts first and thinks later. I've got to keep an eye on him, for Mama's sake. And I meant what I said about making some sense out of Callie's dying. Can you understand that?"

"I guess so."

"So you'll watch out for Mama for me? Keep Tad from driving her crazy?"

54

"I'll try."

They walked on, listening to the sound of their boots on the road, and the rustling of the night creatures in the thicket. When they got home, Pa was standing before the fire, playing his fiddle. Yancy took out his harmonica and began to play a slow, mournful song.

"Don't, Yancy," Mama said. "It's too sad. I can't bear it."

"All right. How about this one?" And he played a faster tune.

"Dance for me, Jessie," Pa said. "It might be a while till I'm home again. I'd like to remember you dancing." And he laughed his happy, reckless laugh.

So Jessie danced.

6

The PROMISE

When Jessie reached the bridge the next morning, Angelina was already there, huddled next to the fire. "What kept you, Jessie?" she asked. "And why such a sad face?"

"I had to help Mama do the washing." Jessie warmed her hands above the flame. "And Pa and Yancy are leaving to join the Texian army."

"Oh." Angelina dropped her gaze. "Then they are enemies of General Santa Anna."

"Oh, why does everyone want to fight?" Jessie cried. "Why can't everybody just share Texas? Lord knows it's big enough!"

Angelina shrugged. "Papa always says people fear those they do not understand. Besides, General Santa Anna is very angry because the Texans ran General Cós out of Texas. Papa says General Santa Anna will never forgive them for causing such dishonor. He is a proud man."

"Can't somebody talk some sense into Santa Anna?" Jessie asked. "Surely no one wants to fight."

"It doesn't matter what the people want," Angelina said. "The general means to teach the Texans a lesson." She took Jessie's hand. "I'm afraid for you, *amiga*. And for your papa and brother. Last night, my uncle Juan came to the house. He says the army will move across the river within days. When that happens, none of us will be safe."

"What are we to do?" Jessie asked.

"If I were you, I would run," Angelina said. "That's what we're going to do."

"I wish you wouldn't go!" Jessie cried, squeezing Angelina's hand.

"I don't want to go, either," Angelina said. "I cried all night. So Papa promised to let me ride with the *vaqueros* once we reach Uncle Julio's *rancho*. He says they can always use more help with the cattle. But we must take care my mama doesn't find out!" Then Angelina brightened. "Enough gloomy talk. Look, I brought you another surprise from Mama's kitchen."

"Another soapy pillow?" Jessie guessed, her mouth already watering.

"*Sopaipilla*," Angelina corrected. "No, this is something different. But I think you will like it."

Eagerly, Jessie took a big bite. "Ahhhh!"

It was so hot Jessie's eyes teared. Her tongue, her very skin, seemed to be on fire. Without thinking, she jumped into the icy river and came up gasping.

On the bank, Angelina bent double with laughter. "Jessie, you look so funny!"

"That was mean," Jessie said, hauling herself onto the mossy bank. "It hurts! And the river is freezing."

"I'm sorry," Angelina said, wiping her eyes. "I should have warned you, but you gobbled it so fast there wasn't time. Here, let me help you."

After they squeezed the water from Jessie's clothes, Angelina piled more wood on the fire. "Sit here and get warm."

Shivering in the cold, Jessie took off her shoes and stretched her stockinged feet toward the fire. Then Angelina asked, "Why don't you wear the necklace I gave you?"

The shame inside Jessie burned hotter than her tongue. How could she tell Angelina? "I didn't mean to, but I lost it."

"I'm sorry," Angelina said. "It was a present from Antonio. He gave it to me the year before he died." She sighed. "That Antonio! What a tease he was. Of all my brothers, he was my favorite."

Jessie knew what Angelina meant. Of course, she loved Tad with all her heart, but Yancy was her favorite. He always seemed to know when she was angry or sad or needed to talk. He never laughed at her feelings, or thought she was silly. Now he was going away.

Angelina went on. "One day, Antonio fell madly in love. Her name was Carmelita and she lived on a farm, on the road to San Felipe."

Spellbound, Jessie crouched by the fire, her freezing toes and damp clothes forgotten. Angelina knew how to tell a story.

"Antonio went to her father, to ask if they could marry, and her father gave his permission. Our families prepared for a big wedding. But it was not to be."

"What happened?"

"One afternoon, on his way home from Carmelita's, something spooked his horse. The horse bolted, and Antonio fell. By the time Papa and my brothers found him, he was dead. I cried for weeks. I couldn't stop."

Jessie nodded.

"After that, I went almost every night to the top of the hill near our house to watch the stars come out. It was summer then, and I would imagine I could see Antonio, smiling at me. I always wore his necklace, so I would not forget him."

"You shouldn't have given me something so precious!" Jessie cried. "If I'd known, I never would have taken it."

"I wanted you to have it. I hoped it would remind you of happy times with your little sister. Perhaps it served its purpose."

"But you didn't even know me that night," Jessie said.

"Your heart was broken," Angelina said simply.

The fire had burned down. Jessie's dress was still damp, but it was time to go.

"Will you come tomorrow?" Angelina asked. "I promise: no more hot surprises."

Jessie grinned and put on her shoes. "I'll be here. If Mama doesn't skin me alive when she sees this dress."

"Be careful," Angelina warned. "There may be soldiers around."

Together the girls smothered the fire. When Jessie got home, Pa and Yancy were in the yard with two horses. On the porch lay two saddlebags, stuffed with powder horns and shot bags and a spyglass.

"There you are!" Pa seemed not to notice Jessie's bedraggled appearance. "What do you think of this horse, Jessie girl?"

"He's not as big as Diablo."

"He's got a good temperament, though. I've been thinking. When this fight is over, he's all yours."

"Mine?" Jessie stared, thunderstruck. Pa was full of surprises, most of them troublesome. But a horse of her very own was a genuine wonderment. Yancy stood there, holding his horse's bridle, grinning down at her.

"Why not?" Pa's brown eyes shone. "You can ride him to school. Teach him some of those ten-dollar words you like so much."

"Thank you, Pa! What's his name?"

"Haven't had him long enough to think one up," Pa said. "Reckon I'll just call him 'horse' and you can give him a rightful name when I come back." He lifted his hand as if to touch her shoulder, but let it fall. "Well, then."

Mama called them to supper. After they had eaten

she brought out a pie. "I let it bake too long," she said. "The crust is too brown."

"It looks fine, Mama." Yancy took a mouthful. "It crunches. What's in here, anyhow?"

"Pecan nuts," Tad said. "I helped Mama crack the shells."

"It's real good, Ruth," Pa said. "Cut me another piece."

It *was* delicious, Jessie decided, even though it looked strange. Then she got an idea. She smiled to herself.

After supper, Tad stretched out on the rag rug with Star and his jackstraws. Mama read her Bible. When the fire burned low in the grate, Pa said, "Me and Yancy will be leaving before sunup in the morning, so we'll say good-bye now."

He hugged Tad and planted a swift kiss on Jessie's cheek. "Help your mama," he said. "And don't be scared. We'll be back before you know it, and then we'll get our farm. You'll see."

"Be careful, Pa," Jessie said, her voice choked with tears.

Then Yancy hugged her, and Jessie knew her heart would break in two. "Don't forget your promise, Jess," he whispered. "This time, it's me who's depending on you."

"I won't forget," Jessie said. "But Yancy, promise you'll come back safe. Promise."

"Have I ever let you down?" He tugged on her braids. "I'll be back, cross my heart and hope to—"

"Don't say that!"

That night, Jessie tried to sleep, but every time she closed her eyes, she worried. She worried about Santa Anna and his army. What if he decided to teach the Texians a lesson while Pa and Yancy were away? Who would look after them then? She worried about Pa. But most of all she worried about Yancy.

When morning came, Pa and Yancy were gone. Tad was still asleep, curled beneath his blankets with Star. Mama was sitting by the window, absently fingering the mending in her lap. Jessie dressed and braided her hair. Then she wrapped a piece of Mama's crunchy nut pie in a clean cloth and hurried to the bridge.

Angelina wasn't there. A hard wind whipped the water into whitecaps. A horse and cart clopped over the bridge. Church bells clanged. Someone shouted. Shivering inside her shawl, Jessie waited as the sun rose higher, sending shafts of feeble light onto the quiet water. Angelina wasn't coming, she decided. Disappointed, she made her way across the moss-slicked bank.

"Jessie!" Suddenly Angelina was running toward her, bracelets jingling, her black curls flying. "I thought I had missed you!"

"I thought you'd already gone," Jessie said. "But I'm glad you're here." She handed Angelina the small square of cloth. "I brought you a surprise."

"For me?"

"Try it!" Jessie waited impatiently while Angelina took a big bite.

"Oh, it's good! What is it?"

"Just something from my mama's kitchen." Jessie waved her hand as Angelina took another bite. "It's her specialty. Fried grasshopper pie."

"Grasshoppers? Ahh!" Screwing up her face, Angelina threw herself onto the ground and scooped water into her mouth. "Ohhh!"

It was Jessie's turn to laugh. Angelina stood up, her eyes wide. Then she laughed till tears rolled down her cheeks. "Oh, Jessie. What a rotten trick! But I had it coming, I think."

"Yes, you did!" Jessie declared. "My tongue still feels hotter than Hades in August. What was that, anyway?"

"A chile my mama calls *quebrado*. She stuffs them with *chorizo* and fries them in lard. Mama knows a thousand recipes for chiles. *All* of them are hot!" Angelina's expression went serious. "I came to say good-bye, Jessie. We are leaving tomorrow and I must help Mama pack."

"I wish you weren't going so far away," Jessie said.

"Me, too. But remember? I drew you a map, in case we ever got to ride with the *vaqueros*."

Taking up a stick, Jessie made an X in the dirt. "This is Liberty. Near the Louisiana border. Right?"

"*¡Justo!*"

Beside the X, she made a squiggly line. "This is the river Trinidad, and here"—she drew another squiggly

63

line—"is the river Sabine. The land between the rivers is the *rancho* Dos Rios."

"Uncle Julio can ride to Liberty in a single morning if the weather is good, and his horse is fast," Angelina said. "If only you could visit me there."

"I wish I could. But we're staying here till Pa and Yancy come back."

"When this is over, we will come back," Angelina said. "And then I will tell you stories of all my exciting adventures with the *vaqueros.*" She took Jessie's hands. "Promise that no matter what happens, you will always think of me as a friend."

Jessie's throat closed up. "I promise."

"Go on, then," Angelina said.

"You first."

Angelina cocked her hip. "It's my bridge. I make the rules. Go now, Jessie."

Jessie gathered her skirts. Without looking back, she raced along the riverbank, then up the hill to the road. The sun had gone and the sky was gray. The wind in the winter-stripped trees made a sound like weeping.

7

THIRTEEN DAYS

Jessie woke with a start. Outside, the sky was still peppered with stars. She sat up, listening to strange echoes in the dark. The very air seemed restless. Drawing her blankets around her, she tiptoed past Mama's bed and went out to the porch. In the distance, dim lights flickered. Wagon wheels creaked, people shouted, horses' hooves clattered over bridges. The Mexicans were leaving.

Jessie's insides shivered. Maybe she should have told Mama about Angelina's warning about Santa Anna's army, but what could Mama do? She ran up the road to watch the Mexicans pass. Along the muddy road came a long line of wagons, their wooden wheels squeaking and groaning.

"Jessie!" Mama shouted into the darkness. "Where are you?"

Jessie ran back to the house. Mama stood on the

porch, her nightgown billowing like a white sail, her stubby candle flickering. "What are you doing out here? You scared me out of my wits."

"The Mexicans are leaving, Mama. What should we do?"

They went inside. Mama lit the lantern and the room glowed with light. Tad stumbled in, holding Star. "What's happened, Mama? Why is everybody up?"

"Sit down, Tad, and listen carefully." Moving quickly, Mama set the tea kettle on to boil. "Remember when Mr. Atterbury said if we were in danger to go to the Alamo?"

"I remember." Tad climbed into Pa's chair.

"We must go there right away, and wait for your father and Yancy to come for us."

"Are the Mexican soldiers coming?" He looked so small, sitting in Pa's chair, his bare feet dangling above the floor.

"I think so."

"Can Star come with us?"

Mama sliced bread and set out a jar of jam. "I suppose so, if you promise to watch out for her. I won't have time to help you."

Just then came a knock at the door.

Mama called, "Who is it?"

"Jimmie Massey, ma'am. From the general store."

He came in, his eyes still droopy with sleep. "Miz McCann? Colonel Travis's scouts have spotted the Mexican army just eight miles out of town. I promised your mister I'd look after you till he gets back, but you'll be safer at the Alamo. I'll wait while you pack your things, but I'd be obliged if you'd hurry."

"Will Davy Crockett be there?" Tad asked. "Can I meet him?"

"He's there, all right."

"Will you have some tea while you wait?" Mama asked, already setting out another cup. "No more questions, Tad. Finish your breakfast and get dressed."

While the storekeeper sipped his tea, Jessie helped Mama gather their blankets and clothes, and the Bible that had journeyed with them all the way from Kentucky. She also packed her warm shawl, her book, and her red hair ribbons.

The sun was coming up as they piled onto Mr. Massey's wagon. Tad held tightly to Star as they rumbled toward the Alamo. The horses plodded through deep ruts in the muddy road, past the deserted plaza, past rows of adobe houses standing empty. The bells in the church tower began a furious clanging that echoed across the deserted streets. As the wagon turned onto another street, Jessie saw the Texian soldiers scurrying toward the Alamo.

"Yah!" Mr. Massey urged the horses on, nearly colliding with a man on horseback riding at breakneck speed down the empty road. Behind him on the saddle blanket rode a young woman holding a baby.

"Almeron Dickinson!" Mr. Massey called out.

The man looked up, saw the wagon, and yelled, "Follow me!"

Jessie clutched the side of the wagon as they splashed across a ford, the water swirling above the wagon wheels and the horses' bellies. The gates swung open and they entered the Alamo.

"You'll be safe now." Mr. Massey jerked his head toward a falling-down building along one wall of the enclosure. "The Mexican artillery can't break through here."

Mama said, "Thank you for looking after us."

"Glad to do it, Miz McCann." He tipped his beat-up hat. "Don't worry. This thing won't amount to much. Once Colonel Travis's reinforcements arrive, we'll send Santa Anna back across the river once and for all."

The mission buzzed with activity. Cannons rattled over the courtyard. Along the high walls, soldiers strode back and forth, peering into their spyglasses. Others nailed together wooden platforms for the guns, or piled dirt against the walls. In one corner of the courtyard, two men hammered apart horseshoes and turned them into ammunition for the cannons. A tall man wearing spurs and a long knife ran back and forth, shouting orders to everyone.

"Who's that?" Tad asked.

"That's Jim Bowie," Mr. Massey said. "He and Colonel Travis are in charge here."

The woman who had ridden in on horseback came over to Mama, carrying a tiny girl on her hip. They had the same dark hair and bright blue eyes. "Susanna Dickinson."

68

"Ruth McCann." Mama reached for the baby. "What a darling child! May I?"

"What's her name?" Jessie asked.

"Angelina Arabella," Mrs. Dickinson said, placing the baby in Mama's arms.

Tad said, "Hey, Jessie. She's got the same name as that girl who came to our wagon that night, remember?"

"It's a common name in these parts," Mrs. Dickinson said. "You stick your head out the door and yell 'Angelina!' and ten little girls come running. So her daddy and I call her Bella instead."

"How old is she?" Mama asked, patting the child's thick curls.

"Fifteen months," Mrs. Dickinson said. "And into everything."

Tad yanked on Mama's skirts. "Can I go find Davy Crockett?"

"No. You stay right here and keep out of everyone's way."

Then another man rode through the gates. A young boy came to take his horse. "Mr. Bonham?" the boy asked. "Did you find Colonel Fannin? Is he coming to help us?"

Mr. Bonham slid from his horse and slapped its flank as he handed over the reins. "I found him, all right. But he's not coming."

Jessie's stomach lurched. There were only a few men inside the Alamo. Even she could see they needed all the help they could get.

69

"Don't joke, Mr. Bonham," the boy said. "We can't fight the whole Mexican army by ourselves."

"I wish I *were* joking." Mr. Bonham took off his hat and wiped his brow. "I'll tell you one thing, son, this army is in one heck of a shape. Fannin claims he's in charge, Grant and Johnson both claim they're in charge. And while they're arguing about who should get the glory, this whole town is being overrun. I wish I'd stayed in South Carolina."

"Excuse me, sir," Jessie said, shifting her small bundle. "Did you see my pa and brother? Luther and Yancy McCann?"

"Sorry, miss. I didn't. I wasted all my time trying to convince that bullheaded Fannin to get his men over here before it's too late." He jammed his hat onto his head. "'Scuse me. I'd best break the news to Colonel Travis."

Then a rosy-cheeked man with thick brown hair and merry blue eyes strode across the courtyard. "Welcome, ladies!" he said. "You seem to have brought all your worldly goods, but if I have my way about it, we'll all be home by tomorrow." He bowed. "Colonel David Crockett."

"You are not," Tad said.

Laughing, the man bent to Tad. "Reckon this will convince you?" From his pocket, he pulled a worn coonskin cap and set it on Tad's head.

"Mama!" Tad cried, clutching the cap with one hand and Star with the other. "It is him!"

Then a single musket ball pinged against the walls. Everyone stood still, listening.

"Come on!" Colonel Crockett said, ushering them across the courtyard. "Let's get you inside."

"Is it safe in here?" Mrs. Dickinson asked. "Almeron said so, but—"

"Safest place in all of Texas!" the colonel said. "Old Santa Anna will have snakes to eat before he gets over that wall." He led them to the chapel, where a small group of Mexican women huddled with their children. Eagerly, Jessie scanned their faces, hoping that somehow Angelina might be among them. But they were all strangers.

One of them came forward, holding the hand of a young boy. "I am Ana Esparza," she said quietly. "This is my son, Enrique. The others don't speak English, but they want me to say we are on the side of the Texians. My husband, Gregorio, is here to help Colonel Travis."

Another musket ball whined overhead. Bella looked stunned, then wailed. The McCanns sat on the cold floor, their bundles at their feet. "I'm scared," Tad whispered to Jessie.

Colonel Crockett said, "You ladies just rest easy now while me, Bowie, and that young fellow Travis figure out how to defend this garden spot of the world without getting us all blowed to Kingdom Come."

"Colonel!" Mama cried. "How can you joke at a time like this?"

"Well, ma'am, back when I was fighting with General

71

Jackson, I learnt that, sometimes, joking about danger is the only way to keep from going plumb crazy."

The colonel left, and the little group fell silent. Then, a rumble from a distant cannon rocked the courtyard. The second burst of fire exploded against the walls and sent a hail of stones and dirt raining down. Jessie pressed closer to the wall and squeezed her eyes shut.

The ground beneath them quaked. But no one spoke.

The battle raged on. Jessie lost track of time. Clinging to Mama and Tad as the din filled her ears, she felt as if days passed. But it was only a single, long afternoon, an afternoon filled with the crack of muskets and the booming of cannon fire, with noise, then silence, and her growing fear.

Toward evening, the fighting suddenly stopped. The soldiers built fires in the courtyard, laughing and talking as if nothing had happened. Emerging from their hiding place, the women went about preparing supper, as if cooking for an army was something they did every day. Soon the smells of peppered beans, tortillas, and sizzling meat filled the air. After supper, Colonel Crockett played his fiddle, the notes rising and dancing in the dark. The soldiers took out their pipes and relaxed, happy that the Alamo still stood. Happy that everyone was still alive.

Davy Crockett finished a reel and set aside his fiddle. "Me and my Tennessee boys went up that ramp this afternoon to see just how many troops old Santa Anna was a-aiming to throw at us," he said. "First thing I know, here comes a scout in his red coat and blue britches, riding along the river toward the west wall. Well, sir, I pulled back on Old Betsy and let him have it, right between the eyes."

"Good!" Tad said. "That'll show 'em!"

"Don't, Tad," Mama said. "That soldier has a family somewhere. Think how sad they'll be."

"It's sad, all right," Colonel Crockett said. "And I didn't aim to make light of it, ma'am. But the Mexican government keeps changing the rules and making up new ones. And folks like you, who came here in good faith aiming to settle, don't know which way to turn."

"Our people were here first." Mrs. Esparza spoke quietly. "It's frightening to see your land overtaken by foreigners."

"Then why are you here?" Jessie felt helpless, swept along by things she couldn't understand. Politics and war. Right and wrong. Good and evil.

"Mexico is our mother country," Mrs. Esparza said, "but San Antonio is our home. Santa Anna intends revenge on all those who brought dishonor to his army. He doesn't care that he will destroy his own people, too. We *Tejanos* have as much to lose as you do."

"Colonel Crockett!" Tad said. "Can I be a Tennessee boy?"

The colonel smiled down at Tad, his blue eyes full of light. "Can you shoot a gun?"

"Mama won't let me, till I'm older."

"Well, I reckon that's a good idea. You're kind of small for this job. But when you're growed up some, I'll see what I can do."

"By that time, the fighting will be over," Tad said. "There won't be nothing left to do."

"Let us hope so." Colonel Travis stood up, warming his hands before the fire. He was younger than Pa, with thick red hair and flashing eyes that made him look very . . . *dashing,* Jessie decided. He wore a pistol and a knife in a holster at his side. "In the meantime, I want the women and children back inside the chapel. Our enemy is setting up batteries not four hundred yards outside the walls."

"Colonel." Mama stood up and brushed the dust from her dress. "Is it true that Colonel Fannin refused to come to our aid?"

"Don't worry. I'll bring him around. And I'm still hoping for help from Gonzales. All is not yet lost. Take your children inside, and try not to worry."

For Jessie, the days inside the compound passed slowly, as alike as beans in a bowl. Some days there were rumors that aid was coming from Gonzales; some days that Colonel Fannin would come from Goliad to help them. Every day was full of battle sounds, the boom of cannon fire and the whine of bullets, the scrape of boots along the barracks floor, the shouts of the sentries keeping watch from the bell tower.

February ended, and March came, and still they

waited. To pass the time, Jessie often read her book in the plaza. Sometimes she played with Star. Once she wove a crown for Bella from the new grass growing along the banks of the water ditch. In the evenings she helped prepare the meals.

One day, a few men from Gonzales stole past the Mexican sentries and slipped inside the Alamo. For the rest of the morning, the compound buzzed with hopeful news from the outside. Jessie was sitting in the courtyard when Colonel Travis came by.

"Jessie McCann, isn't it?" the colonel asked, bending down. "What are you reading?"

She held up her book so he could see the cover.

"*Adventure Stories for Boys and Girls,*" he read. "Sounds exciting."

"Oh, it is!" Jessie said. "But I've read the whole thing three times since we came here. I wish I had something new."

He laughed. "Perhaps I can help you out."

In a moment he returned from his quarters with a thick book bound in brown leather. "Try this one."

Eagerly, Jessie read the title. "*The Last of the Mohicans* by James Fenimore Cooper." She looked up at the redhaired colonel. "What's a Mohican?"

"Read and find out," he said. "Let me know if you like it, won't you?"

Minutes later, Mr. Bonham thundered through the south gate, hanging low over his sweat-lathered horse. He dismounted and stomped into Colonel Travis's office. Closing her new book, Jessie pressed close to the window to listen.

"Bad news, Will," Mr. Bonham reported. "Fannin finally decided to help us, but he got bogged down just outside Goliad. For somebody who went to West Point, he ain't got the sense God gave a goose. Started out without enough provisions to keep a bird alive and had to turn back. There's nobody to help us now. We're on our own."

8

REMEMBER *the* ALAMO

Like fires across a haymeadow, Mr. Bonham's news spread through the compound, stunning everyone into silence. Huddled with Mama and the others inside the chapel as night came down, Jessie tried to read her new book, but she was too scared to concentrate. Mama read her Bible, teased Tad about wearing Colonel Crockett's cap, and wove the red ribbons into Jessie's braids, pretending that nothing had changed. But Jessie wasn't fooled. Nothing in their lives was ordinary now.

After a long while, Mrs. Esparza spoke up. "They say Colonel Travis has asked for help from the governor. Perhaps there is still time."

"We must never give up hope," Mama agreed. To Mrs. Dickinson she said, "Stop your tears, Sue. You're tiring yourself out. Let me take the baby for a while."

Mrs. Dickinson passed her daughter to Mama. "I wish I'd never come here."

"Me too." Jessie's teeth chattered, and she pulled her blankets tightly around her shoulders. "I wish I'd never *heard* of Texas!"

Outside, musket balls pinged against the stone, and the Texians' cannon rumbled a reply. In the courtyard, someone shouted an order, and soon Jessie heard the sounds of running feet, and the clatter of the wooden ladders as they were raised against the walls. Star shot from Tad's lap and disappeared beneath a pile of rubble.

The door swung open and Colonel Travis strode in. "Are you all right, ladies?"

"So far," Mrs. Dickinson said. "Colonel, will no one come to our aid?"

"I've appealed to the governor, to Sam Houston, to Colonel Fannin, to anybody I could think of. It seems we've been forgotten." He looked intently at each of them in turn. "Santa Anna will soon make his move. When that happens, I'll need all my men. I can't spare anyone to look out for you. Can any of you shoot a gun?"

"I can," Mrs. Esparza said. "I used to hunt with my papa."

"I'll give it a go," Mrs. Dickinson said. "How about you, Ruth?"

Mama blinked. "I don't know."

"You're a religious woman, Mrs. McCann," the colonel said. "But believe me, our enemies will show no mercy. If they get inside these walls, you'll have no choice. May I count on you?"

"I'll try."

"Good. I'll send young Fuqua to show you how to load and shoot. In the meantime, pile up all these stones, and anything else you can find. When the fighting starts, stay here, no matter what."

"Cannon fire!" someone yelled from the courtyard. With an earsplitting roar, the cannonball slammed against the wall, splintering the wooden door. Jessie covered her ears. Bella wailed.

"Poor child." His expression thoughtful, Colonel Travis removed his cat's-eye ring. "Would you lend me a ribbon, Jessie?"

She wanted to keep it, because it was a present from Pa, but she couldn't refuse the colonel. Carefully, Jessie untied her red ribbon. Colonel Travis threaded his ring onto it and placed it around Bella's neck. "There now. A pretty plaything for a pretty little girl." He kissed the baby's cheek. "Keep it for me."

His gaze traveled around the dim chapel. "We have only two choices now. Liberty or death. But every day we hold the Alamo buys more time for the Texas army. Even if we lose, in the long run, the better men will prevail."

"How will we know when the battle starts?" Tad asked.

"When Santa Anna gives the order, there won't be

79

any doubt. We'll know. Whatever happens, do your best for God and Texas."

He left the chapel, his boots ringing on the dirt floor. In a few minutes a boy about Yancy's age came in carrying an armload of muskets. "I'm Galba Fuqua," he said. "Pay attention. Here's how these things work."

Jessie watched his hands move as he talked about how to pour the gunpowder from the powder horn into the barrel and tamp it down. Once, he caught her eye and smiled, and she smiled back. He had a way of smiling with his eyes that reminded her of Yancy.

Galba finished his instructions. "Any questions?"

When no one spoke, he stood up and wished them good luck. Then the heavy chapel door swung shut behind him, bringing in a blast of icy air.

"Weather's changed," Mrs. Dickinson said. "Norther's coming in. It'll be cold tonight."

And so it was. Jessie was so cold she thought her fingers and toes would snap right off. Pressed close to Mama and Tad beneath their blankets, she listened to the shouts of the soldiers in the barracks, and the cannoneers rolling the twelve pounders into place. The courtyard echoed with the sounds of men assembling their ammunition, the clatter of horses' hooves as the soldiers led their mounts to the pen, the scrape of metal as bayonets were readied.

"Don't they ever sleep?" Mama asked. "It seems they've been awake for days."

"They can't keep this up forever," Mrs. Dickinson said. "They'll have to rest sometime."

"That's just what Santa Anna is waiting for, I bet," Tad said. "He's going to wait till we're asleep and then he'll attack. But you just wait. Davy Crockett will have them running like scalded dogs."

Just then the door flew open, and Colonel Travis came in with some soldiers carrying Colonel Bowie on a cot. Mr. Bowie's face was so still and pale, Jessie feared he was already dead. But then she saw the faint rise and fall of his chest beneath his blanket.

"Mr. Bowie!" Mrs. Dickinson cried. "Are you all right?"

"I'm afraid not," Colonel Travis answered. "His lungs have given out, and that fall from the scaffold the other day was worse than he let on. I'd like to leave him here, if you're willing to look after him."

The men carried the cot into the corner. As they set it down, the blankets moved, and Jessie saw a whole row of pistols, and Mr. Bowie's knife, hidden beneath his covers.

Mr. Bowie opened his eyes and looked around until his gaze came to rest on Jessie. "What's your name?"

Jessie's voice trembled as she spoke her name.

"I had a daughter . . . but she died . . . back in 'thirty-three. My pistol. Where's my pistol?"

The feel of his weapon seemed to make him stronger. Raising himself onto one elbow, he said, "The

Mexicans may kill me in this bed, but I aim to take a bunch of them with me when I go."

"All this talk of killing!" Mama cried. "It's sinful! And it won't solve anything."

"You're wrong," he said. "It's the only thing Santa Anna understands, and the only way to win the freedom Texas needs." He lay back and reached for Jessie's hand. "Be brave, Jessie."

Mama tucked Jessie and Tad inside her quilts. Then she set her musket on the floor at her feet. "Lie still and you'll soon get warmer."

"What about you, Mama?" Jessie rubbed the goose bumps on her arms. "Aren't you cold?"

"I'm all right." Mama kissed them both. "Try to sleep now."

Through a gash in the thick wall, a sliver of light shimmered from the fires burning inside the Alamo. The sky was inky black and full of stars. For the first time in days and days, the guns were stilled. All was silence and shadows, as if the old mission itself waited for what would happen next. Jessie closed her eyes and finally slept.

Before sunrise, she awakened to the deafening blast of a bugle, and then the sound of thousands of drumming feet across the frozen ground. From somewhere just outside the walls, a band began to play, a scary kind of battle song that seemed to freeze her blood. Above the insistent blaring of the bugle, the musket balls began their assault, slapping against the walls, bouncing off the stone, and rattling across the hard-packed floor.

"Come on, men! The Mexicans are upon us!" Colonel Travis's voice echoed in the darkness. "Man the cannons and fire at will!"

Tad sat up, rubbing his eyes. "I told you so! I *told* you they'd wait till we were asleep. Mama, where's your musket?"

"You leave that gun alone," Mama said. "Colonel Travis and Davy Crockett know what to do."

"Where's Star?" Tad asked frantically.

"Hiding, I am sure," Mrs. Esparza said. "Don't worry, *muchacho*. She will be all right."

Tad climbed onto a pile of rotting timbers and shinnied up the wall.

"What on earth?" Mama shrieked. "Tad, get down from there. Right this minute."

"I can see real good from up here," Tad said. "There's a crack in the wall."

"There'll be a crack in your head when a musket ball comes through there," Mama scolded. "Come down, Tad. I mean it."

"Just a minute, Mama. I can see Davy Crockett and the Tennessee boys. They're guarding the stockade wall."

"Let me see," Jessie said. But Mama pulled her away.

"Can you see my Almeron?" Mrs. Dickinson cried. "Is he all right?"

Tad pressed his face to the crack in the wall. "I can't see nothing now. Oh! There goes Colonel Travis. He's going to help fire the cannons."

Just then the ground rumbled, and the chapel door creaked. With an ominous snicking sound, the Mexicans' musket balls thundered past. Clouds of black smoke drifted across the courtyard. Jessie's eyes burned.

The Texians' cannon thundered a reply, and a great cheer went up.

"Blam!" Tad yelled. "Davy Crockett is firing Old Betsy just as fast as he can load her. I'll bet he kills the whole Mexican army with that gun." He dropped to the floor. "Give me your musket, Mama. Let me go help Davy."

"Hush, Tad! I've told you. We'll have no part of killing."

"You're already a part of it, whether you want to be or not," Mrs. Dickinson said. She held up one hand. "Shhh! Listen."

"I don't hear anything," Jessie said, puzzled. "It's gone quiet as stone."

"God be praised!" Mama said. "Oh, Jessie. The guns have stopped."

"Santa Anna has given up!" Jessie cried. "Can we go home now, Mama?"

Tad did a little wiggle dance there in the middle of the rubble. "I told you we'd whip 'em. I knew we'd win."

Weak with relief, Jessie leaned against the icy wall. At last, it was over. As soon as Pa and Yancy got home, everything in her world would come right again. Maybe Pa would get the farm, or maybe they'd go back to Hickory Creek. With Pa, a person never knew what would happen next. But none of that mattered, as long as they were safe.

Suddenly, a shout went up. Tad peered through the crack. "Mama, come quick. Look!"

"What is it?"

"The Mexicans have broken through the wall!"

"Hurry!" Mrs. Dickinson shouted. "Get your muskets ready. You too, Ruth. This is no time to be pious."

Jessie held on to the musket while Mama, her hands shaking, poured in the gunpowder. Mrs. Esparza finished tamping down the powder in her gun and handed the ramrod to Mama. Mama picked up the musket, her sad gray eyes calm and steady.

Another volley of musket balls flew past, snapping in the frigid air. Grapeshot rained down like hailstones, littering the floor. Through the gaping hole in the wall, Jessie saw Davy Crockett standing in the middle of the gunfire, calmly reloading Old Betsy, his bleeding arm dangling at his side. Mexican soldiers swarmed into the courtyard, their bayonets fixed. The Texians fought back with swords and knives, using musket butts as clubs.

Everything was red, the Mexicans' battle flags, the morning sky, the Texians' blood seeping slowly into the frosted soil. Smells of blood and smoke and gunpowder clogged Jessie's throat. When the Mexican soldiers captured the cannons and turned them on the Texians' sandbag barricades, the screams of dying men echoed in the smoke-filled courtyard.

The chapel door was thrown open and the last of the

Texian soldiers stumbled in. Jessie recognized one of Davy Crockett's Tennessee boys, Billy, and Galba Fuqua, who staggered in, holding his jaws with both hands.

"Galba!" Jessie yelled. "Are you all right?"

He couldn't speak. Blood dripped from his shattered jaw, and he collapsed on the floor at her feet.

"It's all over!" Billy cried. "We're down to scrap metal and rocks for the cannons, and the Mexicans are *still* coming. We've lost!"

Mama's musket slipped from her hands. She closed her eyes.

"What about Colonel Travis?" Jessie asked. "What about Davy Crockett?"

"Colonel Travis is dead. I don't know about Crockett. Last I saw of him, he was still defending the stockade."

Just them some Mexican soldiers burst in. They fired at Colonel Bowie. Billy raised his gun to fire, but a bullet struck him from behind, and he toppled onto Colonel Bowie's blood-soaked cot. Jessie's legs went soft. Now the Mexicans would kill her too. And Mama, and Tad, and all the rest. Her whole body went numb and then she was beyond fear, beyond feeling anything at all.

Then a Texian soldier rushed over to Mama. "Jacob Walker, ma'am. From Nacogdoches. If you get out of here alive, would you take a message to my wife? Would you tell her . . ."

Before he could finish, a Mexican soldier ran toward them, his bayonet at the ready.

"Mama!" Jessie yelled. "The musket!"

But Mama stood still. Seizing the musket, Jessie aimed and fired. The musket slammed against her shoulder, but the shot missed and lodged in the stone wall. The soldier ran his bayonet through Jacob Walker, tossing him into the air like a rag doll. His blood spattered onto Jessie's face, warm as summer rain.

Empty of all thought and feeling, Jessie stood there, not breathing, not seeing. Mama was crying, but made no sound.

An officer in a tattered uniform came over to where they huddled against their terror and the bitter cold. "Señoras," he said gently. "I am to escort you to the house of Ramon Musquiz. There you will wait for General Santa Anna."

"Santa Anna!" Mrs. Esparza spat.

When Mama looked doubtful, Mrs. Dickinson said, "It's all right, Ruth. Mrs. Musquiz is a friend."

The officer motioned them toward the door. "Come."

He led them out of the chapel and through the smoldering courtyard. Everywhere Jessie looked were crumpled soldiers and bent bayonets, broken muskets and blackened clothing. One of the cannons, blasted from its platform, lay on its side on the edge of the wall. A broken knife rested blade-down in the dirt. The icy wind sent pieces of a map tumbling across the frozen ground till they caught on a dead soldier's boot.

Holding tightly to Mama's hand, Jessie passed

9

SANTA ANNA

through the gates, then along the road to an adobe
house. It was Sunday morning. The sun was rising.

Mrs. Musquiz waited for them in the yard.

"Sue!" she cried when Mrs. Dickinson appeared. "Thank Heaven you're alive! How is the baby?"

"She's all right." Still dazed, Mrs. Dickinson waved her hand toward Jessie and Mama and the others. "These are the McCanns. Ana Esparza, Enrique . . ."

"Never mind the introductions," Mrs. Musquiz said. "Come inside. General Santa Anna will soon be here."

While they waited, Mrs. Musquiz washed the blood from Jessie's face. No one spoke. Her ears ringing in the sudden silence, Jessie watched the fire dancing in the grate, glad to be alive, glad to be sitting before a warm fire. She thought of Pa and Yancy, glad they hadn't come to the Alamo. Even Colonel Fannin's men couldn't have lasted long against thousands of Mexican soldiers. Maybe now Pa would see how foolish it had been to come here. Maybe he would take them home to Kentucky and forget his impossible dreams.

"Señoras!" A Mexican officer strode into the parlor and bowed to them as if they were at a ball. "I am General Antonio López de Santa Anna."

Jessie stared at the fierce, dark-haired man. He wore an elaborate uniform with a red and blue sash and miles of gold braid. On each shoulder was a ball of gold, with gold fringe hanging down. He stood before them, unsmiling, and tall as a tree. Then he spied Bella and his expression softened. "What a lovely child! My officers tell me her father perished with the others. That is regrettable, senora."

Mrs. Dickinson drew the baby closer. "We'll be all right."

"Tell me. Did those foolish men really think they could win?"

"It's happened before," Mama said quietly. "The Bible is full of examples. But I don't suppose a man like you concerns himself with religion."

"That's not true, señora. I pray every morning."

"For what?" Mama asked, her voice thick with tears. "For more muskets and cannon?"

"Ruth," Mrs. Dickinson warned.

Jessie leaned back in Mrs. Musquiz's chair and closed her eyes. She wanted to crawl into her own warm bed and sleep until Pa and Yancy came back. But Santa Anna didn't seem to be in any hurry to release them.

"What happened today is only the beginning, unless you are willing to submit to the authority of the Mexican government, and give up this ridiculous fight for independence. You cannot possibly win."

Jessie remembered Colonel Travis's last words to them. *Every day we hold the Alamo buys more time for the Texas army.* A hot, angry feeling bubbled inside her.

"You just wait!" she blurted. "When Colonel Fannin finds out what you did, he'll make you wish you'd never even heard of the Alamo."

Santa Anna's black eyes bore into hers. "I would not depend upon Fannin if I were you, little one. He lacks the stomach for battle."

From a leather pouch, he took a handful of silver coins and handed them around. "Buy food for your babies," he said. "My men will bring you some blankets. Then I would advise you to get out of Texas. As a favor to Señora Musquiz, I have spared your lives, but I cannot be responsible for your safety."

At the door he turned back to Mrs. Dickinson. "Perhaps you will return a favor?"

"After all you've done to us, you beg a favor?"

"I beg for nothing. I *request* that you take a message to the people at Gonzales. Tell them what happened this morning at the Alamo. Tell them many others will die unless they stop this rebellion."

He turned and went out. The very walls around them sighed with relief. Mrs. Esparza and her children knelt before the fire and said a prayer. When Mama began to weep, Jessie went to her and laid her head on Mama's shoulder.

"What will we do now, Mama?" Tad asked, his voice small and scared.

"I don't know. I'll have to think about it."

"Are Pa and Yancy coming back?"

"I don't know."

"Are we staying here, or are we getting out of Texas, like the general said?"

"Hush, Tad! Don't ask so many questions." Mama's voice broke. "I can't think."

"Ruth." Mrs. Dickinson set the baby on the floor. "We

91

can't stay here. Almeron has a cousin in Gonzales. Please. You and your children come with me."

Mama seemed dazed. "Gonzales?"

"It's not that far. If the soldiers haven't taken our wagon, we could use it. We could leave now."

"What about those soldiers? There must be hundreds of them, swarming over this town."

"They're too busy celebrating to care about a wagonload of women and children. Besides, Santa Anna practically ordered me there. No one would dare contradict him."

Mrs. Esparza spoke up. "There are many in Gonzales who believe General Santa Anna is in the right. Tell the soldiers you are going there to spread word of their conquest. They will let you pass."

"What about you?" Jessie asked. "Where will you go?"

"San Antonio de Béxar is our home." Mrs. Esparza drew her children close. "We will stay, whatever comes."

Bella began to cry and Mrs. Dickinson picked her up. "Please, Ruth," she said, her voice wobbly. "I can't take any more. Let's get out of here."

"I want to go home first," Mama said.

"There isn't time! We should leave now. Before Santa Anna changes his mind."

Just then, two soldiers threw open the door and strode into the house carrying blankets. "Compliments of the general," said one. "Stay warm, señoras."

When they left, Mrs. Musquiz said, "My son will help you hitch your wagon, and I'll give you some food for the journey, though there isn't much. The general helped himself to everything but our plough horses. You're welcome to a team."

An hour later, they started for Gonzales, the wagon creaking and jerking over the frozen ground. Huddled inside her blankets, Jessie was overcome with a weariness as wide as Texas. She couldn't remember the last time she'd eaten. She was no longer sure what day it was. All she knew for certain was that she was now on another long road, with little left to rely on.

The wagon clattered across the bridge where she had once played with Angelina, and Jessie's heart burned for a friend so quickly made and quickly lost. For if they ever met again, it could never be the same. Not after the Alamo.

"Stop!" Tad cried suddenly.

"What is it?" Jessie asked.

"Star is still inside the Alamo! We have to go back."

"We can't go back, Tad," Mama said tiredly. "You know that."

"But Mama," he protested. "What if the Mexicans find her? They'll kill her, just like they killed Mr. Walker." He sobbed.

"Don't cry, Tad," Jessie said. "She'll be all right."

"How do you know?"

"She's smart. She'll find a safe place to hide, and when we come back, she'll be right here waiting. You just wait and see."

"But who will feed her?" He wiped his face.

"She can catch mice. She can take care of herself."

The wagon rolled on. Soon they came upon a group of Mexican soldiers marching along the road. As the wagon trundled past, some waved and shouted, some took off their hats. Jessie couldn't tell whether they were being respectful or mocking them. She kept her eyes on the toes of her scuffed shoes. Mrs. Dickinson murmured, "Should I stop?"

"Not unless they insist," Mama said.

"How much longer?" Jessie asked, when long shadows lay across the rutted road. "I'm exhausted."

"Four days, if we're lucky," Mrs. Dickinson said. "Almeron and I once made the whole trip in three and a half, but he was a better driver than I am." She halted the wagon in a clearing beside the road. "I don't know about you, Ruth, but I can't go another mile."

"No sense in wearing everyone out," Mama agreed. "See to your little one, Sue. I'll unhitch the team."

"I'll help you." Tad jumped to the ground.

Jessie followed, with a stew pot and the vegetables Mrs. Musquiz had sent. While Tad and Mama unhitched the horses, Jessie went to the stream for water. Mama made a fire and tossed carrots and potatoes into the pot.

Tad pawed through the food basket. "Did that lady give us anything sweet?"

"Some dried peaches, and a few apples," Mrs. Dickinson said.

Tad grabbed a handful of peaches. Seizing his grubby hand, Jessie said, "Put those back! Do you want to starve to death before we get to Gonzales?"

"But I'm hungry now! And anyway, we'll be in Gonzales in no time."

"Maybe," Mrs. Dickinson said, glancing up. "I don't like the looks of that cloud."

"Creation!" Jessie grumbled. "That's all we need. As if we're not miserable enough already."

"Jessie." Mama took her arm. "Stop complaining. Be thankful you're alive. Now, who's hungry?"

"Me!" Tad said. "I'm so hungry I could eat a horse!" He glanced at the team, grazing in the shade. "I don't mean you!"

"Oh, Tad." Mrs. Dickinson laughed. "If you're not a caution! I don't see how your mama gets anything done with all your monkeyshines."

"He takes after his pa," Mama said. "Always full of mischief."

The last light drained out of the sky. As the stew warmed her insides, Jessie grew quiet. It seemed a thousand years had passed since the McCanns had come to Texas. It was hard to remember what her life had been like before Callie died, before she and Mama and Tad had gone to hide inside the Alamo. She missed Pa and Yancy. She wished they were here now, to listen to her story and keep her safe.

In the distance, thunder rumbled. "We'd better finish," Mama said. "Sounds like we're in for some rain after all."

"We'll be drier under the wagon than inside it," Mrs. Dickinson said.

The trees swayed in the wind and the lightning made

golden cobwebs across the dark sky. Then the clouds cracked open and the rain blew in, cold and sharp as broken glass.

"My legs hurt," Tad complained the next morning. "And I'm about to perish. Can I have some peaches, Mama?"

"Not yet, son. Wait till we're nearer the end of the trip."

Tad's face wore a mutinous look. Jessie said, "Listen, Tad. I know what we can do. Let's ration our food. Like Texian soldiers."

"What's ration?"

"Divide it carefully, and eat a little bit at a time. So we won't run out before we get to Gonzales."

"Are Pa and Yancy rationing, too?"

"I'm sure they are." Mama smiled and smoothed his tangled hair. "Would you like a story? It might take your mind off being hungry."

"All right."

From beneath her shawl, Mama brought out her Bible. Tad's eyes widened. "I thought the Mexican soldiers took all the Bibles."

"All but this one. I hid it inside my bodice."

Mama chose the story of David and Goliath. When she finished, Jessie donned her shawl and went down to the river for water. Looking toward the horizon she saw a great brown cloud rising from the earth.

"Mama!" she called, sloshing the water from her bucket as she ran back to the wagon. "Look at that!"

"What in the world?" Mama asked.

"Must be the wind, stirring up the dust," Mrs. Dickinson said.

"Not likely with all the rain we had last night."

As they watched, something caught the light. A sword? The barrel of a musket? Jessie's breath caught. "It's the Mexican army!" she cried.

"Quick, Jessie," Mama said. "Pick up those blankets and put out the fire. Tad, help me with the horses."

While Mama and Mrs. Dickinson hitched the team, Jessie tossed their blankets and cooking pot into the wagon. Everyone piled inside.

"Get up!" Mrs. Dickinson yelled to the team, and the wagon jounced along the muddy road. The whip cracked the air. The wagon bounded along, sending Jessie and all their belongings flying. Only Bella seemed to think it was fun. She squealed and clapped her hands every time the wagon hit a bump in the road.

To keep her mind off the soldiers and the jerking, bone-rattling ride, Jessie thought about the three things she wanted most. First, a good hot dinner. Some ham, maybe, with gravy and hot corn pone, and for dessert, one of Mama's custard puddings with cream. Then, an honest-to-goodness house with windows and doors and a roof to keep the rain out. Most of all, she wanted Yancy and Pa to come back and fill up the empty places their leaving had made. If only Pa would come and find her, she would never complain again. Pa could keep his crazy schemes and his card games, too, if that's what he truly wanted.

When they reached Gonzales, late on the fifth day, the town was in an uproar. People rushed around, shouting to one another. Houses stood empty. Coils of rope, bundles of bedding, baskets and barrels, shovels and buckets littered the road. Teams of oxen were hitched to wagons and carts of all descriptions.

Mama halted the team and everyone jumped off the wagon.

Mrs. Dickinson stopped a woman rushing past. "What's happened?"

"You haven't heard?" the woman said. "The Mexicans have overrun the Alamo. Killed every last man. Everybody's headed east, to Louisiana."

"But that's hundreds of miles from here!" Mrs. Dickinson said.

"Listen," the woman said. "I'm sorry. I have to go. If you're smart, you'll do the same."

Mrs. Dickinson stood still, tears shimmering in her eyes. Mama slumped against the wagon wheel. Never had they seemed so defeated.

"Excuse me, ma'am." A man in a soft-brimmed hat stood smiling down at Mama. "I couldn't help overhearing. My name's Wyatt Austin. Is there anything I can do to help?"

Mama and Mrs. Dickinson took turns telling Mr. Austin about the Alamo. When they told him about that last morning, when all the Texians were killed, he took off his hat and held it over his heart. "And you ladies are the only survivors."

"Us and a few *Tejano* women," Mrs. Dickinson said. "And a couple of servants. Thank God for Mrs. Musquiz. We owe her our lives."

"I knew most all those fellows from Gonzales," Mr. Austin said quietly. "I'd have gone to the Alamo with them if I'd gotten back from San Felipe in time."

"We hoped to find shelter here," Mama said. "We're worn out."

"We just got word from General Houston," Mr. Austin said. "He's given us the army's wagons and advised us to abandon Texas. It's not safe for anyone here now. Our only chance is to outrun the Mexicans. They won't dare follow us into United States territory."

"But we're traveling with children!" Mama protested. "Isn't there some place we can rest?"

"I'm afraid not. The Mexican army could show up here any minute. I don't have to tell you what will happen to any Texian standing in their path. You're welcome to join my family," Mr. Austin said. "My wife and daughter are right over there."

Jessie looked where he pointed. On a wagon piled high with crates and baskets sat a sunken-eyed woman, and a girl with dark curls spilling out of her bonnet. The girl lifted her head and smiled. Jessie felt a little better.

"I came here to find my husband's cousin," Mrs. Dickinson said. "Lottie Mason."

"Tom and Lottie left town more than a week ago," Mr. Austin said. "They were the smart ones, I reckon. None of us thought Santa Anna would bother with the Alamo."

"We were outnumbered," Jessie put in. "We fought hard. But nobody lifted a finger to help us!"

"What a horrible spectacle for children to see." Mr. Austin bent down to her. "You mustn't think about it anymore. It's over now and we have to go on the best way we can."

"We can't keep going with hardly any clothes and nothing to eat." Mrs. Dickinson said. "I counted on Tom and Lottie to help us. Now I don't know what to do."

"Wait here." Mr. Austin strode away. He stopped several men on the road, nodding his head toward the spot where Jessie and the others waited.

Soon a crowd gathered, offering blankets, dry clothes, bits of food.

"Is it true?" asked a grizzled old man in a beat-up hat. "Were you really inside the mission when it fell?"

"Yes," Mama said quietly. "I'm afraid so."

"How perfectly thrilling!" a pock-faced woman cried. "You must write a story about it."

"It wasn't thrilling," Tad said, his bottom lip quivering. "It was scary. The Mexican soldiers kept on shooting everybody even after they were dead. They killed Colonel Bowie even though he was in bed and too sick to fight back. And I had to leave my kitten, too." He burst into tears.

"Oh!" said the woman. "You poor little thing. I only meant—"

100

10

The RUNAWAY SCRAPE

"Never mind, Lucinda." Mr. Austin bent to Tad. "Don't cry, son. You must be brave for just a while longer. Can you do that?"

"I don't know."

"You look pretty tough to me. Your ma and sister are counting on you to be the man of the family."

"I don't *like* being the man of the family."

"I know what you mean," Mr. Austin said gravely. "Sometimes it's a genuine trial." To Mama he said, "I'd drive this wagon for you myself, but my wife's been sick. She's too weak to manage a team."

"It's all right," Mama said. "We've come this far on our own. We'll manage."

"I'll be right behind you." He tossed another bundle into the wagon. "It's a long way to the border. We'd better get going."

They set out toward the river, a caravan of wagons and sleighs and carts. Jessie counted nearly fifty wagons on the road heading east.

Before they had gone very far, sunset came, then early twilight, purpling the sky. The air crackled with cold, and a yellow half moon hung large and low in the sky. The wagons rolled east until the horses' heads dropped and even the sturdy oxen began to balk.

When at last Mr. Austin signaled for a stop, the travelers drew their wagons into a ragged circle on the dry prairie. The men made campfires, and after a hurried meal, the weary travelers bedded down for the night.

Huddled beneath their blankets, Mama sang to Tad and Jessie, her voice soft in the dark. Jessie stared up at the sea of patient stars, wishing hard for Pa and Yancy.

"Jess?" Mama whispered. "Are you awake?"

"Yes, Mama."

"I'm sorry I failed you when the Mexican soldiers started shooting. I wanted to fire that musket, but I couldn't. I'm proud of you for being so brave."

"I wasn't brave," Jessie said. "I was scared. I didn't want to shoot anybody, either. I just wanted the fighting to stop."

An owl hooted. The insects made little ticking sounds in the dry grass.

"And I miss Pa and Yancy," Jessie said, swallowing the lump in her throat.

"They'll be back soon. You'll see."

"How will they know where to find us?"

"Maybe Colonel Fannin will know where we've gone. But if he doesn't, once we're safe in Louisiana, I'll send word to Pa myself. You mustn't worry about it. Try to sleep now. Tomorrow will be another long day."

In the morning, the caravan started out while it was still dark. Then the rain came. The wagons bogged down in the mud, but the travelers dared not wait for the road to dry. Everyone got out to help push the wagons out of the mire. While Mrs. Dickinson held the reins, Mama, Tad, and Jessie put their shoulders to the wheels and heaved. The horses snorted and shied in their traces. The wagon creaked.

"Push, Jessie!" Mama cried. "It's starting to move!"

Jessie strained against the heavy wheel until she feared her bones would snap. The cold rain poured into her eyes and down her neck. Thick, red mud oozed into her shoes. At last the wheels caught and turned. Mrs. Dickinson guided the horses out of the mire and into the line of shivering trees along the road. They climbed back into the wagon. Mrs. Dickinson took one look at them and giggled.

"What's so funny?" Mama asked.

"Look at your face!" she said, shaking with laughter. "Jessie's too! You look like two drowned rats!"

Mama wiped the mud from around her eyes, making two white circles in her red-spattered face. "You should see yourself, Sue Dickinson! You look as if you just walked out of a pig sty!"

Mrs. Dickinson pulled clumps of muddy goo from

her sopping hair. "Oh, mercy! Don't we make a picture? I'm glad Cousin Lottie wasn't here to see it. She always said any woman who engages in physical labor is not quite respectable."

"My teacher said a true lady can make anything respectable if she keeps her dignity while she does it," Jessie declared, wiping the grit from her mouth.

"How can I keep my dignity when my hair is plastered with mud?" Mrs. Dickinson said.

"Pretend you're an Egyptian." Tad looked up from his whittling. "They used to do it all the time. To dye their hair."

"Is that a fact?" Mrs. Dickinson's smile was very white against her muddy face. "Where did you learn that, Tad?"

He shrugged. "In a book. I'm hungry. When can we eat?"

"Not for a while yet," Mama said. "Mr. Austin wants to make the ferry crossing at San Jacinto before nightfall."

"Nightfall? That'll take forever!" Tad groaned and fell onto the pile of blankets.

Mama eyed him sharply. "Are you all right, Tad?"

"I dunno." He scratched his arm. "I feel kind of funny."

Jessie stared at him. "Creation! You're red as a beet. What are all those little red bumps?"

"Bumps?" Mama asked. "What bumps?"

"On his forehead," Jessie said. "Look."

"Oh, mercy!" Mama said. "I hope it isn't measles."

"Maybe he ate too many dried peaches," Jessie said. "Or maybe it's poison ivy."

"Maybe it's just plain old mud!" Tad said, frowning. "It does itch, though."

"Take your shirt off," Mama said.

"It's too cold, Mama."

"Just for a minute, son."

His chest was peppered with red bumps, too.

Mama slumped on the seat. "It is measles. I'm sure of it. When we stop tonight, I'll see if Tad and I can ride with somebody with no children. Maybe the Austins will let Jessie ride with them. No sense in making everyone sick."

"But Mama, I don't even know the Austins," Jessie said. "I want to stay with you."

"Don't fight me, Jess," Mama said. "I'm too tired."

"You'll be all right, Jessie," Mrs. Dickinson said. "As soon as Tad is well, you can come back."

"When my friend Ellen got the measles, she didn't come to school for three whole weeks!" Jessie said. "We'll be clear to Louisiana by then!"

They rumbled over a rickety wooden bridge, and at last came to the place Mr. Austin called the San Jacinto. Jessie could scarcely believe her eyes. She hadn't expected to see thousands of wagons that stretched out along the banks of the river, waiting to cross on the ferry. The noise was deafening. Planters with their slaves, and merchants with wagonloads of merchandise,

105

fought to be the first ones to cross. Harnesses jingled, wagons clattered, guns boomed, sending a fearsome racket echoing through the trees.

People and animals, wagons and carts, poured onto the ferry. Suddenly, someone shoved Jessie from behind and she sprawled into the mud. Before she could pick herself up, a girl's voice said, "Are you all right?"

It was Sarah Austin. Jessie stood up, wiping her stinging palms on her skirt. "I think so."

"These people are so rude," Sarah said. "But Father says your mother and Mrs. Dickinson are ladies."

Remembering how they'd looked pushing the wagon out of the mud, Jessie grinned. "You wouldn't have believed it today. We were all working like field hands."

"Don't I know it!" Sarah said, her expression merry. "I tripped twice on my hem before the whole waist of my dress ripped right out. Mother was fit to be tied."

Sarah treated the whole episode like an adventure. Jessie hoped Mrs. Austin wouldn't mind if she rode with Sarah in the wagon.

"My brother has the measles," she blurted out. "Mama wants me to ride in your wagon so I won't catch them too."

"Really?" Sarah seemed delighted. "I was hoping for a chance to make friends with you. I'm sure Mother won't mind, as long as we don't mention the part about the measles. She's been so sick she just can't bear to think about disease."

"Should we ask your father?" Jessie wondered.

"Oh, he won't mind. He spoils me silly." Sarah flashed a smile. "It comes with being the only child, so I've decided to enjoy it." She looped her arm through Jessie's. "Come on. Let's go tell Mother. Then we'll get your things."

They found Mrs. Austin in the wagon, propped against her pillows. In her pink striped dress and white lace collar, she looked sweet as a dumpling. Engrossed in her book, she seemed oblivious to the confusion swirling around the jammed river crossing.

"Mother," Sarah began. "I'm so bored I could just scream. May Jessie ride in our wagon to keep me company? Please?"

Mrs. Austin frowned at Jessie. "Have you some dry garments, dear?"

"A few," Jessie said.

"Well, get them. And then find some place to clean yourself up. You too, Sarah. Cleanliness is next to godliness. Don't forget that."

"No, Mother. We won't." Sarah winked at Jessie.

"And Jessie. I'll expect you girls to be quiet while I'm trying to rest. I've not been well."

"I'll be quiet," Jessie promised.

"Where will you go once we're out of Texas?" Jessie asked on the evening of the third day. There were only four or five wagons ahead of them now. Tomorrow they would cross the river and continue their journey.

Sarah looked up from the cap she was knitting. "I don't know. Father says maybe New Orleans."

"I've been there," Jessie said. "Once."

"Truly? What's it like?" Sarah's needles stopped clicking. "I've heard there are places where ladies dance in fancy costumes, and they don't wear a single stitch underneath!"

"Sarah!" Mrs. Austin said. "Such talk!"

"Well, that's what I heard," Sarah said. "Did you see any dancing ladies, Jessie?"

"No." Jessie told Sarah about the day they'd arrived on the steamer from Louisville, the ladies in silk dresses on the bustling pier, the soft-colored houses and the towering church spires. "And Pa bought us some pastries sprinkled with sugar," she finished.

"If we settle there, you'll come and visit me," Sarah decided. "Father will buy me a carriage with fine horses that run like the wind. We'll go riding every afternoon."

Mr. Austin looked up from the map he'd been studying. "No matter where we wind up, you'll be going to school, young lady. You won't have time for racing around in a carriage."

"Oh, pooh! I don't need any more schooling," Sarah declared. "I can read and write as well as you and Mother. I can sing and play the piano, and look." She held up her half-finished cap. "I've even learned to knit. Honestly, Father, I'll learn more by observation than I ever could in some stuffy old schoolroom. You said yourself experience is the best teacher."

Mr. Austin smiled at his daughter. "What a cunning little creature you are."

Sarah laughed, and her tiny teeth shone like pearls. "But you love me, Father. Admit it. Aren't I your favorite person in the whole world?"

"You and your mother." He folded his map. "But I still intend you to have a proper education, Sarah."

"Oh, pooh," Sarah said again. But she smiled into her father's eyes with such delight that Jessie knew she wasn't really cross with him.

Watching them made Jessie's heart ache. If only Pa would come home, she would try harder to make him love her the way Mr. Austin loved Sarah. She would be so perfect that Pa would never again do anything to vex her or embarrass her. The McCanns would live happily ever after, just like the Austins.

They heard a noise outside the wagon. Mr. Austin picked up his pistol.

"What is it, Wyatt?" Mrs. Austin asked, rising from her pillows.

"Stay put. I'll check."

Sarah said, "Do you suppose it's Indians? Wouldn't that be thrilling?"

"Terrifying, if you ask me," her mother said.

"Oh, pooh," Sarah said. "Indians wouldn't be half as terrifying as the fight at the Alamo. Did you shoot anybody, Jessie?"

109

"Don't be silly," her mother said. "Of course she didn't. And your father warned you not to bring up such a painful subject. Now, let's talk about something more pleasant."

"Pleasant?" Sarah frowned. "Let's see. So far we're running for our lives from the very Mexicans that captured the mission, we've bogged in mud, we've slept in these hard wagons so long I could positively scream. We've been bitten by bugs, and poor Jessie was nearly trampled by some dolt who pushed her into the mud rather than wait his turn like a gentleman. Yes, Mother. I'm sure if I put my mind to it, I can certainly conjure many pleasant subjects upon which to remark."

Mrs. Austin rolled her eyes. "Tell me, Jessie. Do you speak to your mother this way?"

Before Jessie could figure out how to answer that question, Mr. Austin returned. "Nothing to worry about. Just a couple of men who had too much to drink. I sent them off to bed."

"It's time we all turned in," Mrs. Austin said. "Tomorrow will be a busy day."

And so it was. In the morning, Mr. Austin led five wagons onto the ferry. Jessie and Sarah stood at the edge of the flatboat, daring the water to lap onto the tops of their boots. Behind them came men on horseback, and Negro slaves carrying carts and barrels loaded with belongings. The flatboat rocked on the silvery water as it slid away from the shore. When they reached the other side, the wagons formed a line again and they set off through the timber, heading for the next river.

"How much farther to Louisiana, Father?" Sarah asked. She and Jessie were riding on the wagon seat next to him.

"Too far yet to talk about," Mr. Austin said.

"I know why you said that," Sarah declared. "You think if we knew how many miles are yet to be crossed, we'd get discouraged. Aren't I right, Father?"

"Something like that. When a problem seems too big to hold in your mind all at once, it's best to think about it in small parts. Take it one step at a time. Instead of thinking about how far it is clear to Louisiana, we'll think about getting to the next river and then the one after that. Before you know it, we'll be back in the United States of America."

"And away from Santa Anna," Sarah said. "Tell me, Jessie. What does he look like? Is he really as fierce as they say?"

"Sarah," her father said.

"Oh, all right. I don't see why I'm not allowed to talk about him."

After Jessie described the general, Sarah said, "He doesn't sound so ferocious to me. Father could beat him in a wrestling match any day of the week."

"Thank you for that vote of confidence," Mr. Austin said. "But I hope I never meet up with him."

When they reached the river called the Trinity, they

came upon a group of soldiers from the Texas army. Jessie hurried to help make camp, and when the fires were lit and the beef was boiling in the pots, everyone gathered to hear the latest news.

The one who called himself Captain Daniels said, "Last we heard three days ago, the Mexicans were crossing the Colorado River."

"The Colorado?" Mr. Austin said. "That's it then. We're finished."

"We're retreating, all right, but we're not giving up yet. There are still plenty of men left willing to fight for independence."

"That's right," said a tall, prune-faced man from Gonzales. Jessie had seen him several times, riding his horse in front of the wagons. "I aim to get my family safely into Louisiana, and then I'll be back to help you boys fight to the finish."

"What about Colonel Fannin?" Mr. Austin asked. "I understand he's gathered more than four hundred men."

In the flickering firelight, Jessie's eyes met Mama's. At last, some news of Pa and Yancy.

"Colonel Fannin and his men were taken prisoner," Captain Daniels said. "They're being held at Goliad."

Prisoners! Jessie's heart jerked.

"Are you sure?" Mama asked.

"Yes, ma'am. That's what I heard. Try not to worry. Now that the Mexicans have won the Alamo, maybe Santa Anna will order their release."

"He won't," Mama said sorrowfully. "He means to crush us all."

Remembering her promise to Yancy, Jessie put her arms about Mama's shoulders. "Don't cry, Mama. Tell me about Tad."

"He's getting better," Mama said. "We're riding with some folks from San Felipe till it's safe to go back with Sue and the baby."

Captain Daniels stirred the fire and poured himself more coffee.

Jessie stood up. "Captain, will the Mexicans let the prisoners go soon?"

"Hey! Hey! River's rising!" Men shouted in the darkness. "It's washing over the banks."

Everyone rushed toward the river. In the flickering torchlight, Jessie counted eight ferrymen struggling to keep the boats from breaking their moorings. "Families with sick children first!" one yelled. "Hurry!"

"Mama, that's you!" Jessie cried. "You must take Tad across."

"I can't leave you here," Mama said. "I'll wait for the Austins."

From the shadows, Mrs. Dickinson said, "You may as well come with me, Ruth. Bella's got the measles too. I want to cross as soon as I can."

"Go on, Mama," Jessie said. "I'll be safe with the Austins."

"How will I find you on the other side?" Mama asked. "There must be at least a hundred wagons here."

"Don't worry, Mrs. McCann," Mr. Austin said. "Jessie has become as dear to us as our own daughter. We'll look after her for as long as it takes."

Jessie felt tears starting. Why couldn't her own pa be more like Mr. Austin? Sensible and responsible. Grown up.

"Thank you, sir," Mama said to him. "I'll look for you on the other side."

The crossing was scary to watch. The first group of wagons rolled onto the ferry just as the river broke over its banks. From the shore, Jessie watched the black water swirling around the ferry, stranding the travelers. People shouted. Horses whinnied.

"What should we do?" she cried to Mr. Austin.

"Nothing we can do," he said. "Except pray for this blasted river to go down."

Throughout the long night, Jessie waited with the others. As dawn broke, the ferrymen turned the boat around and started across. The water swirled and eddied around the ferry. From her perch on the wagon seat, Mama waved her handkerchief till the ferry disappeared around a curve in the river.

One trip. Two trips. Three. At last the Austins' wagon rolled onto the ferry and they made the slow journey across the river. On the other side, Mr. Austin flicked the reins and they splashed across the waterlogged lowlands, setting off once more for the wide prairie. Day after day, the caravan rolled eastward. Soon, food became scarce. More people got sick with measles and cholera. Those who died were buried quickly, for no one knew when the Mexican soldiers might appear.

One evening, Mr. Austin halted the wagon at the crest of a low ridge and pointed to a small town in the distance. "If my map is correct, that's the town of Liberty."

Liberty. Somewhere close by was a ranch called Dos Rios, and Angelina. Part of Jessie ached for her friend, but she hardened her heart. She wouldn't think of it now. She was hungry and bruised, and anxious for news of Mama and Tad.

"I hope we can find a decent bed for Lydia, and rest these horses for a couple of days before we push on," Mr. Austin said. "And I hope we can find your mama, young lady. I imagine you're missing her by now."

"Yes, sir."

But so much had happened lately that it sometimes seemed the Austins were her real family and the McCanns were people she'd read about in a book. She watched the darkness spreading out like a thundercloud. Above the wagon, bats circled in the dim sky and night birds swooped in with a soft beat of wings. Far below, in the darkness, a single light gleamed like a tiny jewel.

The inn was overflowing with weary, sweat-stained travelers, but after Mr. Austin offered the innkeeper a handful of coins, beds were made for them in the hall.

"My young friend here is looking for her mother," Mr. Austin told him. "Ruth McCann is the name. She's traveling with a small boy and another woman. Mrs. Dickinson."

"Sue Dickinson?" asked the innkeeper's wife. "Has a baby with her?"

"That's her!" Jessie cried. "Have you seen them?"

"You're in luck," the innkeeper said, rubbing the huge wart on his nose. "They're over at Mrs. Franklin's boardinghouse. You can't miss it. There's a sign at the gate."

"I'll go with you, Jessie," Sarah said.

"No, you stay here and look after your mother," Mr. Austin said. "I'll walk Jessie over to the boardinghouse and be right back."

"Oh, pooh." Sarah pouted for a minute before she hugged Jessie. "I'll see you tomorrow."

Jessie walked with Mr. Austin down the road. Soon they saw candles flickering in the windows of the boardinghouse, and the blue sign rocking in the wind. Before Mr. Austin could even knock at the door, it opened and there stood Mama and Tad.

"Jessie! Thank goodness." Mama hugged Jessie. To Mr. Austin she said, "Thank you for taking care of my daughter."

"It was no trouble. Sarah and Lydia enjoyed her company. Matter of fact, so did I."

Tad was jumping up and down like a wind-up toy. "Guess what, Jessie? I'm all well. See? Only a few bumps left."

"I'm glad." She smiled down at him. "Did you miss me?"

"Nah. Yes. A little."

"More than a little," Mama said. "He asked about you every day."

Mr. Austin said, "We'll be heading east again on Thursday, Mrs. McCann. Unless, of course, Santa Anna's army catches up to us before then. You're welcome to join us. Mrs. Dickinson, too."

"We've spent most of the last six months traveling," Mama said wearily. "I don't know about Sue, but I've had about all I can take. And until I have some word about the prisoners at Goliad—"

"I understand. Maybe you should wait here till there's some definite news. We're not far from the border now. If trouble comes, you can get out quick. Have you heard anything at all?"

"Nothing since we crossed the Trinity."

"Soon as I get my family settled across the border, I aim to come back and help the Texians fight. People are outraged over what happened at the Alamo. If Santa Anna thinks we'll just go away quietly after what he did, he's sadly mistaken. Will you be all right, Mrs. McCann?"

"I suppose. People here are scared, but most are staying put for now."

"I'll say good night then." He tipped his hat. "Sarah will be around to see you before we leave, Jessie."

Mama led Jessie to their room at the back of the

117

house. In a room across the hall, Mrs. Dickinson sat, rocking Bella.

"Will she go on to Louisiana with the Austins, Mama?" Jessie asked.

"I expect so. She has no family to keep her here."

Then Mama folded back the covers and Jessie slept in a real bed for the first time in weeks.

Two days later, Sarah came to the boardinghouse to say good-bye. She wore a dress the color of spring grass, and a sunbonnet with lace around the edges. "I meant to see you yesterday, Jessie, but Mother was too sick." She spun around and around, like a doll atop a music box. "Father bought this for me. Isn't it divine?"

"It's beautiful," Jessie said, fingering the soft folds of the skirt.

"I want to wear it all day. Mother won't hear of it. But I ask you, Jessie, what's the point of having beautiful things if you can't enjoy showing them off?"

Looking up from her mending, Mama said, "You'll have plenty of chances to show it off once you reach Louisiana."

"Do you think so?" Sarah tilted her head. "Perhaps I'll save it for your visit. Oh, you will come to see me, won't you, Jessie? Say you will."

"Maybe someday. If Pa and Yancy . . ."

"*When* Pa and Yancy get home," Mama said firmly. "As they most surely will. You must write to us, in care of Mrs. Franklin's, as soon as you're settled. Perhaps all of the McCanns will pay you a visit some day."

"Sarah!" Mr. Austin's voice boomed down the road.

"Oh. I mustn't keep Father waiting," Sarah said.

Jessie blinked, trying not to cry. It seemed she was always saying good-bye to the people who mattered the most. She and Mama and Tad walked with Sarah out to the road where the wagons waited. Mrs. Dickinson and the baby were in their wagon with some others from Gonzales and a wounded man from the Texas army, going home to Sabine.

"Good-bye, Sue!" Mama called. "God bless you!"

"Good-bye! Good-bye, Jessie. Bye, Tad!" Mrs. Dickinson seemed almost happy. She held the baby up. "Say bye-bye, darling. Say bye to Jessie and Tad."

They waved until the wagons rattled out of sight.

"Well," Mama said. "That's that."

She tried to make her voice bright and shiny, but Jessie knew she was worried and afraid.

In the afternoon, they were sitting on the porch when a dusty rider charged into town. People poured into the road and gathered around.

"Citizens of Liberty!" he cried. "Santa Anna's army has crossed the Brazos River and is heading for Harrisburg."

A man in the crowd spoke up. "Is there no stopping him? This is bad news indeed."

"That's not the worst of it, I'm afraid. I've word of Colonel Fannin's men, too."

Her heart hammering, Jessie pressed forward to hear the news.

11

An UNEXPECTED ENCOUNTER

"Dead? All of them?" Mama clutched Jessie's shoulder.

"Yes, ma'am. It happened last Sunday. They say the Mexicans lined 'em up and shot 'em where they stood. Even Colonel Fannin himself."

"Oh! Oh, Tad!" Mama cried, pulling Tad to her chest.

Jessie felt as if sharp teeth were gnawing at her heart. She looked up at the dusty rider, her fists curled into two hard balls at her sides. "You're lying! They're not dead!"

"Two of my cousins were at Goliad, miss," he said sorrowfully. "I wouldn't lie about a thing like this."

"Miz McCann? Are you all right?" Mrs. Franklin had crossed the street from her boardinghouse, still holding her pie tin.

"I'm all right," Mama said.

But she wasn't. How could any of them ever be all right when their whole life had scattered like leaves in

120

stormy air? Mama's face was so pale, so full of sorrow, that Jessie wanted to say something that would take the suffering out of her. But nothing she could say would fix all the things that had gone wrong.

People began drifting away, talking low, caught up in their own grief.

Mrs. Franklin said, "I am truly sorry, Miz McCann. I sure wish there was something I could do to help you."

"Thank you," Mama said. "But there's nothing anyone can do."

"What will we do now, Mama?" Tad asked. "Where will we go?"

"Hush!" Jessie thumped him on the shoulder. "Don't bother her now! Can't you see she can't think?"

"No wonder," Mrs. Franklin said. "What a terrible shock." She put her arm around Jessie's shoulder, but Jessie ducked away. Her throat ached, and her insides felt raw as an open sore. She couldn't bear Mrs. Franklin's kindness. If she let the woman hug her, she'd start crying and never stop. When they got back to the boardinghouse, Mrs. Franklin sent Tad to fetch wood and water. He tore out of the house, slapping the door back on its leather hinges, as if he couldn't wait to get away.

Mrs. Franklin settled Mama in the parlor. "You just sit here and rest, and don't even try to think. I'm going to make us a nice pot of tea, and a good supper. Tomorrow will be soon enough to sort things out."

She bustled about the kitchen, setting out pots and

pans, clanking the crockery on the wooden table. Tad returned with a bucket of water. It sloshed a little when he set it down. "I left the wood on the porch."

"There's a good lad," Mrs. Franklin said. "Now go and keep your mama company. It won't be long till supper."

In a little while, Mrs. Franklin set out a meal of meat and gravy, potatoes and corn. Everything smelled good, but the food stuck in Jessie's throat. She took a few bites, to be polite, then pushed her plate away and sat staring out the window as night came down.

Afterwards, sitting in the circle of flickering firelight, her skin turned to gold by the flames, Mama seemed quiet and calm, like a marble angel in a cemetery. Opening her Bible, she began to read. " 'Sorrow endureth for a night, but joy cometh in the morning.' "

How could she think that? Jessie wondered. How could they ever be happy now that Pa and Yancy were gone forever?

When Pa talked about the farm he planned to buy, Jessie pictured it in her mind. A sturdy house with plenty of windows to let the sun in. A red barn full of horses and sweet-smelling hay, and beyond the barn, green pastures dotted with fat cows. And down the road from the farm, in the calm shade of towering trees, a school brimming with books, and a teacher who made you think and laugh and learn. And a best friend. But all that was gone now.

"Amen," Mama said quietly, and Jessie started, realizing she'd missed the prayer. It didn't matter. It seemed like you could hope and pray until something burst inside you, but it wouldn't change anything.

"That was a fine meal, Mrs. Franklin," Mama said. "Thank you."

"Oh, my blessed. It's the least I could do."

"Do you suppose the man at the livery stable would sell me a wagon and team?"

"A wagon and team? Good gracious! Surely you're not thinking of setting out alone. Not with the Mexican army on the march."

"We can't stay here forever, imposing on you. I want to go back to San Antonio. All our belongings are in that house. I have to know what's left."

Jessie swallowed the sick feeling in the pit of her stomach. How could Mama even *think* of going back to that sad place?

Mrs. Franklin fluttered around like a small bird, picking up their tea things, banking the fire for the night. "You're not thinking straight, Miz McCann. You've had an awful shock. What you need is a good night's sleep. Things always look different in the light of morning."

"Are we really going home, Mama?" Tad asked, yawning. "I hope so. 'Cause I want to find Star. I hope she's waiting for us, just like Jessie promised."

"We'll see. Go to bed, son."

Jessie lay wide awake, imagining Pa and Yancy marching out to be shot, imagining the feel of the thawing ground turning to mud beneath their boots, the roar of muskets, the sudden flash of gunfire. She turned over on the thin mattress and squeezed her eyes shut.

Mama was crying quietly into her pillow, a wretched, desolate sound that tore at Jessie's heart. Tiptoeing across the splintery floor, she crawled beneath the quilts with her.

"Oh, Jessie," Mama said, "What's going to become of us? What are we going to do?"

Jessie wanted to scream and cry till all the pain and rage were out of her, but what good were bitter tears? She didn't know what to do. But she had promised Yancy to look after their mother. "We'll be all right, Mama. You'll see."

When morning came, Mama seemed to have forgotten her plan to return to San Antonio. She lay in bed, not speaking, not moving, as if she'd built a thick wall inside herself and left everybody else on the other side of it. Hovering in the doorway, Jessie waited and watched, hoping Mama would sit up, smile and say something to take away her fear. But the only sound was the scrape of tree branches against the dusty windowpane and the distant rattle of wagon wheels on the road.

"Jessie," Mrs. Franklin said, coming up behind her. "Let your mother rest. I need some things from the store. Take this list to Mr. Hollis and tell him to put it on my bill."

"May Tad come with me?"

"I've set him to chopping wood. He's better off keeping busy outside. You run on now. You know where the store is. Out past the livery stable."

Jessie took the basket Mrs. Franklin offered. Part of her wanted to get away from the place where the bad news had overtaken them, but she worried about Mama.

"She'll be all right," Mrs. Franklin said. "I've got a nice pot of chamomile tea brewing. It'll help her sleep."

Crossing the brown-stubbled yard, Jessie pushed open the gate. It was still early; morning mist curled through the trees beside the road. She passed the newspaper office, the inn, and finally the livery stable, where two brown horses stood blinking in the growing light. Outside the general store stood a wagon piled high with sacks and crates. An old man leaned against the wall, whittling. He nodded when Jessie came up the steps.

The store was dim and musty. Across the back wall was a counter laden with tins and baskets. Next to a smoky, pot-bellied stove was a half empty barrel of flour. At a table near the window, two women were admiring a bolt of cloth. Jessie listened to their discussion as she moved along the aisles, filling Mrs. Franklin's basket with spools of thread, a dozen candles, a roll of twine.

Then Jessie heard a girl's voice, soft and insistent. "Please. You must let me have these things."

Jessie froze. Peering around the corner, she saw a girl at the counter, a basket of supplies over her arm. It couldn't be, and yet it was! There was no mistaking the tumbling black curls, the saucy red skirts.

Overcome with emotions she couldn't name, Jessie stood where she was, half hidden between a stack of metal buckets and a thick coil of rope. She didn't know what to think. Part of her wanted to embrace Angelina and shout for pure joy. But another part of her couldn't forget the horror of the Alamo and wouldn't forgive the people who had caused it all.

Mr. Hollis, the storekeeper, leaned across the counter, his face dark as a thundercloud. "I told you. It'll be a cold day in July before I sell so much as a thimble to the likes of you. Mexicans aren't welcome here now. So get on out of here. I've got things to do."

"Please." Angelina sounded desperate. "My papa needs these nails. And we are nearly out of food. My uncle Julio has been your customer for years. He told me so himself."

"That was before the Alamo. Things are different now. I don't aim to stand here arguing about it. You put those things back and get going."

Jessie's foot had gone numb. She shook it, and the stack of buckets crashed to the floor.

"Tarnation!" Mr. Hollis cried. "What's going on?"

Angelina whirled around and her mouth dropped open. "Jessie? Jessie McCann? It's really you! Oh, I cannot believe it. What are you doing here?"

Mr. Hollis picked up the fallen buckets. "What the devil were you doing hiding back here, girl? Playing spy?"

Jessie's mouth worked, but no sound came out.

"This is my friend!" Angelina told the storekeeper. "She knows my family has nothing to do with Santa Anna. Tell him, *amiga*. Tell him who I am."

Memories of the Alamo filled Jessie's head. She

couldn't forget the sticky feel of Mr. Walker's blood on her face, the choking smells of smoke and gunpowder, nor the horrifying sight of the Texian soldiers lying broken and bloodied in the courtyard. She could not forget that Pa and Yancy had died trying to help Colonel Fannin defeat Santa Anna.

Angelina waited, her basket over her arm, her eyes pleading.

Jessie felt sick. Suppose Mr. Hollis refused to sell her the things they needed, because she was a friend of the enemy. She had to look out for Mama and Tad. She had promised Yancy. "I never saw her before in my life," she muttered. "She's got me mixed up with somebody else."

"Wouldn't make no difference to me," Mr. Hollis said. "A Mexican is a Mexican, far as I'm concerned."

Angelina flung her basket aside, spilling everything onto the floor. "Uncle Julio will never forgive you for this," she told the storekeeper. She stared at Jessie, her face full of anger and hurt. Then she turned and ran out, slamming the door behind her.

"You see?" Mr. Hollis said to Jessie as he gathered up the sack of nails and a handful of candles that had scattered on the floor. "Bad tempered, every last one of them. Well, what can I do for you?"

Jessie handed him her list and waited while he measured out flour, sugar, and salt, and tied the bags with string. Outside, a harness jingled, and then the wagon, with Angelina at the reins, raced down the road and disappeared into the trees.

12

JESSIE'S CHOICE

About a week later, Jessie was awakened by a sound outside. Tiptoeing to the window, she cupped her hands to the glass and peered out. There stood Angelina, a flickering torch in one hand, a pistol strapped to her waist.

Before Jessie could call out, Angelina put a finger to her lips and motioned Jessie outside. A million questions spun inside Jessie's head. Was this for real, or only a strange, mixed-up dream? Should she go outside? Wake Mama?

She thought of the musket hidden behind the kitchen door, but it was hard to believe Angelina had come to harm her. Maybe Angelina only wanted to scare her, to get even after the incident in Mr. Hollis's store. Jessie didn't know what was right or what was wrong or who to trust. Nothing made sense. Maybe she was only imagining the whole thing. She blinked her eyes. Angelina was still there, the wind whipping her skirts, the torchlight leaping in the darkness. Grabbing her shoes, Jessie crept down the hall, through the parlor, and onto the porch, closing the door softly behind her.

Angelina threw the torch down and ground the fire out with her boot. Beyond the dark trees, a crescent moon peeked from the gray-rimmed clouds. Pale stars winked along the rim of the earth.

Jessie chafed the goose bumps on her arms. "What are you doing here?" she whispered angrily.

"I would not have come, since you have no wish to know me," Angelina said, her words jagged and sharp. "But this is a matter of life and death. I have seen your brother."

"You're lying!" Jessie said. "All the men at Goliad were killed. Even Colonel Fannin himself."

"I am not lying. Two nights ago, I was helping the *vaqueros* with the cattle when I heard a terrible moaning sound in the brush. At first I thought it was a wild animal caught in a trap. But when I came closer, I saw that it was Yancy.

"Colonel Fannin is dead," Angelina went on. "And most of his men, too. But Yancy escaped. He remembered your telling him about Uncle Julio's *rancho,* and he came there to hide from Santa Anna's soldiers. He's hurt, but alive. I swear it."

Jessie eyed the pistol at Angelina's waist.

"You don't believe me."

"How did you know where to find me?" Jessie asked. "And why did you bring a gun?"

Angelina laughed softly. "Liberty is not a big town. When you were not at the inn, I knew you must be here. As for the gun, anyone who travels in the woods at night must have protection from the coyotes. Did you think I came to harm you? We made a promise, remember?"

Jessie swallowed the hard pain in her throat.

"What happened at the mission Alamo was bad," Angelina said. "I had nothing to do with it, but I am trying to make amends, Jessie. Even though you refused to help me when I needed it."

"I'm sorry for that," Jessie said, her face hot with shame.

"We needed those things. Even my mama cannot make bread from stones. But it is done now, and your brother is waiting."

And then Jessie began to believe it was true. "What about Pa?" she asked. "Did Yancy say—"

"He doesn't know," Angelina said. "When the shooting began the men ran. He saw many of them die, but he has no word of your papa."

"Where is Yancy now?" Jessie asked. "When is he coming home?"

"He's too weak to travel alone. I've come to take you to him."

"How can I get him home?" Jessie's teeth chattered in the cold. "We don't have a wagon or a mule. Would your pa bring him here?"

"I cannot ask Papa," Angelina said sadly. "He would punish me if he knew I was here. Papa says Texans cannot be trusted. He says they are greedy for land, and hungry for power."

"Then what can I do?" Jessie cried.

"Your brother is hiding in an empty farmhouse not far from Uncle Julio's," Angelina said. "He needs food, and medicine for his wounds. He needs someone to help him get back here."

Around them, the sky lightened and the stars faded into the gray dawn.

"Hurry!" Angelina said. "I must get home before Papa finds out I'm missing."

Jessie made a choice. If Pa had survived, he would skin her alive for disobeying him, but she had to trust Angelina. She hurried inside. The fire in the parlor had burned down to coals; the ashes made a sighing sound as they settled into the grate. Moving quietly through the sleeping house, Jessie dressed. She gathered food, salve, and a clean towel to make bandages. Taking up the chalk Mrs. Franklin kept for writing her supplies list, she scrawled a note to Mama. *Yancy's alive, I've gone to get him. Don't worry.*

A row of empty glass jars rested upside down on the windowsill. Working quickly, Jessie filled one with flour, the other with salt. In the yard, she handed them to Angelina.

Angelina wrapped them in her shawl. "Come on. The sun's almost up."

They cut through the stand of trees at the end of the road and followed a creek until it emptied into the river. For a long time they traveled silently, running through the long, twisted shadows of early morning. Jessie's lungs burned, and her stomach rumbled. The smell of the food she carried made her mouth water, but she didn't dare eat it. Yancy needed it more than she did. She kept her eyes on Angelina's darting form, not thinking, just putting one foot in front of the other.

When the sun was high in the sky, they waded across a shoal. The cold water swirled around her knees but she hardly felt it. All she could think about was Yancy. For most of the afternoon, they followed an old trail, walking in the hardened ruts made by wagon wheels. When at last they stopped to rest, Jessie wiped her face and squinted into the sun. "How much farther?"

"Not far," Angelina said. "I must leave you at the end of this road, but you won't have any trouble finding your brother."

"Leave me?" Fear made Jessie's voice squeak. "You can't leave me out here!"

"I must get back before Papa finds out I've gone," Angelina reminded her.

Jessie felt her eyes go hot. After all that had happened between them, she couldn't let Angelina go without telling her the truth about something. "Remember the necklace you gave me, the night Callie died?"

"I remember."

"I told you I lost it, but that's not exactly the truth."

When Angelina didn't say anything, Jessie went on. "Pa wouldn't let me keep it. He said I shouldn't trust you. He said you might accuse me of stealing it and send somebody to arrest me."

"And did you believe this thing?"

"Not for a single minute! But he took the necklace away. I was too ashamed to tell you what he said, so I made up the story about losing it."

"I didn't think you had lost it."

They started walking again, their bundles bumping against their legs.

"Mama is planning to take us back to our house in San Antonio," Jessie said. "If I find your necklace, I'll send it to you."

"But who knows where I'll be then?" Angelina said, laughing. "This is a big country. No, if you find it, keep it. Perhaps someday your papa will change his mind about me."

Then the crushing weight of Jessie's sadness settled onto her heart again. "I don't know whether he's alive."

"No," Angelina said. "But as Papa says, miracles are the children of faith. You must never give up hope."

They came to a stand of cane that stretched to the far horizon. Standing on tiptoe, Angelina pointed. "See those trees over there? Where the green turns to gray?"

"Creation! Way over there?"

"Just beyond them is the farm. Your brother is hiding

in the storehouse. We thought he'd be safer there, in case the farmer came back."

"But how will I get there?" Jessie asked. "There's no road. Not even a cart path."

"Walk straight through the cane field. Keep looking up, and you won't lose your way."

"Angelina." Jessie's breath caught.

"I wish I could go with you, *amiga*. But I can't." She took Jessie's hand. "Don't cry. You'll make me cry, too. And how will I explain my tears to Papa? Go on now. Your brother needs you."

"Will I ever see you again?" Jessie asked.

"When we are grown up, come to Mexico City. Ask for the most famous woman in all of Mexico, and someone will lead you to me!"

With a final wave, Angelina turned and hurried down the road. Jessie plunged into the sea of rattling cane. The sun streamed in. Sweat ran into her eyes, and stung the scratches on her hands. She was tired, and hungry, and scared, without Angelina for company. The cane snapped beneath her boots and when she finally looked up, the trees seemed as far away as ever. *One step at a time,* she told herself. *Just like Mr. Austin said.*

At last she came to the row of trees. Beyond them stood the abandoned farmhouse, just as Angelina had promised. Jessie began to run through a weedy field thick with briars and vines, then across the empty yard to the storehouse.

And there was Yancy—dirty, ragged, and bloodied—asleep on the dirt floor.

She stood in the doorway, waiting to catch her breath, staring at the filthy bandage protruding from his shirt collar, and the bruise that spread like an ink stain over his cheek.

He opened his eyes, and a slow smile stole across his face. Jessie smiled back, dazed with joy. She'd waited for this moment all day, but now that she was truly face-to-face with him, she didn't know what to say. Finally, she said, "Is this a dream, or is it really you?"

He grinned. "So, Angelina found you! I've been looking for you forever! Where's Mama? Is Tad all right?"

Jessie threw her arms around her brother. She started talking and couldn't stop.

"I came by myself. Well, with Angelina, but she left me ages ago! I brought you some food and some salve, and as soon as you're well, we'll get Mama and Tad. Mama wants to buy a horse and wagon and go back to San Antonio . . ."

"Whoa!" he said, untangling himself. "Slow down. One thing at a time."

Opening her bundle, Jessie said, "Are you hungry?"

"Hungry as a bear."

He sat up and took the food she offered, chewing slowly, grunting a little with each bite. Jessie touched his bruised cheek. "What happened?"

"Got hit with a rifle butt."

"Does it hurt?"

"Like the devil. Is there any more to eat?"

She tore some ham into small bites for him. At last he said, "That's enough. If I eat too much, I'll get sick."

He shifted on the floor. "How's Mama? And Tad?"

"She's all right. Tad got the measles while we were running from Santa Anna, but he's well now. Yancy, is there any news of Pa? Did he escape, too?"

"I wish I knew. Everything happened so fast."

"Oh, you don't have to tell me! It must have been awful!"

He swallowed hard, and his eyes filled up. "It was Palm Sunday. They said they were letting us go, because Colonel Fannin agreed to surrender. They split us into four groups and marched us out. Some of us went down toward the river, and some went into the trees. We were so stupid, we really thought they meant to let us go."

"Oh, Yancy. Was Pa with you then?"

"No. They took his group into the woods. I heard the guns and said to the guard, 'What was that?' I'll never forget the look in his eyes. He said, 'Oh, they're just killing some beef.' And then he started shooting. I got hit in the shoulder. I fell down, and then me and this other boy, name of Davis, started crawling toward the water. We could hear the grapeshot pounding the trees all around us. When we got to the water, I just started swimming. I don't know what happened to Davis."

Jessie touched his shoulder where the dirty bandage bulged under his shirt. "Is it bad?"

"Bad enough. I sure wish Dr. Wilson was here."

"I brought some salve. And we'll find a doctor in Liberty. Can you walk?"

"Not for very long. I get dizzy." He closed his eyes and sighed. "The last time I saw Pa, he couldn't talk about anything but you, Jess. The Mexicans took that horse he promised you. He purely hated the thought of letting you down once again."

A lump knotted Jessie's throat. Hot, silent tears stabbed her eyes.

"Maybe he got away, too," Yancy said. "Maybe the bullets missed him and bounced off the trees. Maybe he hid in the bushes till it was safe to come out."

"Angelina says we have to hope."

"Ah. Angelina."

"I didn't trust her at first." Jessie sat with her feet out in front of her, watching the dust motes dancing in the air.

"Don't be so hard on yourself," Yancy said. "I was scared to trust her myself. But after Goliad, there was no use going back to San Antonio, so I just kept on going east, toward the United States. Once I got near Liberty, I realized I was near her uncle's place. I figured it might be safer to hide out with Mexicans. And once I was better, maybe I'd meet up with somebody who'd know where you and Mama were."

He rubbed his shoulder. "Ow, that hurts."

"Can I get you anything?" Jessie hovered anxiously above him. "Do you want to lie down?"

"Maybe I'd better."

He settled himself on the floor. Jessie removed his dirty bandage and smoothed some salve into his jagged wound. With the clean cloth from Mrs. Franklin's kitchen, she made a fresh bandage.

"What else can I do, Yancy?" Jessie asked. "Are you thirsty?"

"I could use some water. There's a creek not far from here. And a bucket by the door. Angelina filled it up before she left me here."

When Jessie returned from the creek, Yancy was asleep. She sat on the hard-packed floor listening to his breathing, watching the shadows creep along the walls. She felt calmer than she had in a long time. And happier. Yancy was alive!

Pa was alive, too. He just had to be. He couldn't be dead when she hadn't had a chance to show him she was different now.

Night came, and the rats scurried over the floor, rustling the cornstalks. Jessie curled her feet under her skirts and slept. When she woke, the door was open and the sky was full of light. Yancy was gone. She scrambled to her feet and peered out, just as he ambled out of the woods. "Sorry if I scared you." He jerked his thumb. "The outhouse is down that way."

"Are you better?"

"Not much. This grapeshot is keeping my fever up. We should start home today."

"That's impossible! You can't even walk without getting dizzy."

"But the longer I wait, the worse I'll get. The food you brought helped a lot, Jess. If we go slow, I can make it. I want to see Mama and Tad."

After they'd eaten, they retraced Jessie's trip across the cane field, then along the rutted wagon trail till they reached the deep river crossing. There Yancy folded himself onto the muddy bank. "Wait a minute. I don't feel so good."

Jessie lay on her back, watching the puffy clouds piling up in the sky, imagining the happiness on Mama's face when she and Yancy came strolling into Mrs. Franklin's yard.

"Jessie?" Yancy called. "Come here a minute."

His face had gone pale as whey.

"What's the matter?"

"I feel sick. Help me up."

Yancy was sick in the grass. When it was over, he lay back, breathing hard. Jessie wiped the sweat from his face. "You see, Yancy McCann! I told you we should have waited, but you wouldn't listen."

"Don't get your dander up. I'll be all right. I shouldn't have eaten so much this morning, that's all."

"Maybe we should camp here today," she said. "And go home tomorrow."

"No. The sooner I get to a doctor, the better. We'll

rest here awhile and go on." He let out a shaky laugh. "Wish I had some *aguardiente* right about now."

"What's that?" Jessie plopped down beside him.

"Mexican fire water. They say it's good for what ails you."

"You wouldn't dare! Mama would skin you alive!"

"Pa let me try some once, right after we joined up with Colonel Fannin. But don't you dare tell Mama."

"I won't." Jessie returned his delighted grin, her very insides dancing with happiness. It was just like old times, sharing secrets with Yancy. "What did it taste like?"

"The truth? It's the worst-tasting stuff I've had in all my born days. Hotter than blazes. Burns your throat all the way down."

He leaned on Jessie's shoulder. "Come on. Let's get going."

They walked steadily through the lengthening shadows until they reached the boardinghouse. Tad tore out the door and wrapped himself around Yancy's knees. "You're back! You're really back."

Yancy ruffled his hair. "Of course I'm back, you little rascal. I couldn't break a solemn promise." His eyes met Jessie's over their little brother's head.

"Did you shoot the Mexican soldiers, Yancy?" Tad queried. "Did you have a rifle like Davy Crockett's?"

"We had rifles, all right, but not much chance to use them. Have you been good, Taddie? Did you help Mama?"

Tad nodded, his little face shining with joy. "I was the man of the family. But it's your turn now. I'm too tired."

Then Mama rushed over. "Yancy! Oh, thank heaven you're all right."

Yancy held on, his dark head bent to her gold one, while she sobbed onto his good shoulder. Jessie stood there crying, too.

At last, Mama pulled away. "How did you know he was alive?" she asked Jessie. "Why didn't you wake me instead of running off on your own? You could have been hurt, or captured, and I'd never have seen either of you again."

"There wasn't time," Jessie began. "Angelina—"

"Angelina? That Mexican girl?" Mama's eyes flashed. "How could you bear the sight of her?"

"She saved my life," Yancy said. "I was so weak I wouldn't have lived another day if she hadn't helped me. She gave me food, and brought Jess to take me home."

"You were foolish to trust her," Mama said.

"I know an angel when I see one," Yancy said.

13

PA'S GIFT

"Creation! What a wretched chore this is!" Jessie was up to her elbows in hot, steamy suds. Her knuckles were red from scrubbing against the washboard, and her back felt like a knotted rope. The fire licked at the edges of the black kettle, and clouds of steam puffed into the bright April sky. Behind her, a line of wet clothes flapped in the wind.

"Watch your language, Jess." Mama plunged her stick into the pot, brought out a graying nightshirt and jiggled it in the hot water.

"Well, it *is* wretched. I'm sweating like one of Pa's old plow mules."

Mama smiled. "We're almost finished. Go ask Mrs. Franklin if there's anything else that needs washing, before we let this water cool."

I don't see why we have to work like slaves," Jessie grumbled. "Why can't she boil her own drawers?"

"You know why," Mama said patiently. "We're out of money. Mrs. Franklin is kind to let us stay on here while Yancy is recovering. The least we can do is earn our keep."

"How much longer do we have to stay? I've already missed nearly a whole year of school."

"I can't answer that." Mama tucked a loose strand of hair behind her ear.

Just then, Tad sprinted across the dirt yard, scattering Mrs. Franklin's chickens. "Mama! Somebody's coming."

Jessie shaded her eyes. Down the long, dusty road came a man in a black coat and hat riding a brown horse. Her heart leapt. Maybe it was Pa, coming home at last. But, as the man drew closer, Jessie saw that it was not Pa after all. Then Mama said, "Why, that looks like Dr. Wilson!"

"Mama! It *is* Dr. Wilson!" Tad cried. "From the boat to Velasco! Remember?"

"Of course I remember." Mama dried her hands on her apron. "Go ask Mrs. Franklin to put the coffee pot on, son. And comb your hair."

They waited for the doctor on the porch. He tethered his horse and removed his dusty hat. "Mrs. McCann. I met up with Wyatt Austin last week over near Sabine. He said I might find you here."

"I'm glad you're all right. Yancy survived the massacre at Goliad, but he's not well yet. And we're still hoping for news of my husband."

"Is there some place we could talk?"

Both Mama's hands went to her chest, as if she needed to hold her heart in place. "You have news of Luther?" she asked, her voice wavering. "It's bad, isn't it? Where is he? Is he—?"

"Why don't we go inside."

Jessie followed them into Mrs. Franklin's parlor. Tad had slicked his hair down and was helping set the table. Mama introduced Dr. Wilson to Mrs. Franklin, and explained how they met on the boat to Texas. "Dr. Wilson took care of Callie when she got sick."

"A beautiful baby. So cheerful and full of life." Dr. Wilson hung his hat on a peg and raked his fingers through his hair. "I was sorry to hear you lost her."

Mrs. Franklin poured coffee. "Cream, Doctor?"

"Black is fine." He glanced around the parlor. "Where's Yancy?"

"I'll get him!" Tad trotted down the hall and returned with Yancy.

"Dr. Wilson!" Yancy shook the doctor's hand. "I wondered if you'd survived Goliad."

"I was lucky. General Urrea needed someone to take care of his wounded and decided to spare me. I escaped after the massacre." He sipped his coffee. "How are you, Yancy?"

"Better than I was three weeks ago. I took some grapeshot in the shoulder."

"Yancy," Mama said. "The doctor has some news about your pa."

Mrs. Franklin said, "Why don't we all sit down."

When they were seated in the parlor, Dr. Wilson said, "There's no easy way to break bad news, Mrs. McCann. It grieves me to tell you Luther is dead."

Tad sagged against Yancy. Jessie gripped Mama's hand. She wanted to scream and howl and smash everything in sight. But she sat, still and dry-eyed, staring at the blue cream pitcher on Mrs. Franklin's tray.

Finally Mama whispered, "Are you sure?"

"I'm afraid so. It was over before he knew what hit him."

"Thank God for that," Mama said. "I couldn't bear it if he'd suffered."

"He gave me something for you the night before," Dr. Wilson said. "Seems as if he had a feeling something bad was about to happen."

He handed Mama a thick white paper, folded in half and sealed with red wax.

"What's this?" Mama held it carefully, as if it were a sacred jewel.

"The deed to that farm he promised you when you pulled up stakes and came to Texas. Four thousand acres of prime land, not ten miles from San Antonio."

"That's just like Pa," Yancy said bitterly. "Biting off more than he can chew. How does he think Mama and I can make payments on a place that big?"

"It's all paid for, Yancy. It's yours. Free and clear."

"That's impossible," Mama said. "Where would Luther have gotten that kind of money?"

"I promised I wouldn't tell you," Dr. Wilson said, "since he said you wouldn't approve. But I can't see that it matters now."

Mrs. Franklin stood up. "More coffee, Doctor?"

"Don't mind if I do." He waited while she refilled his cup. Then he said to Mama, "Truth is, he won that land playing monte."

"He *gambled* for it?"

"Now don't go getting upset. The fellow who owned it said it had become a pure trial to him. He wanted to get out of Texas and go back East where he came from. Luther did him a favor by taking it off his hands."

"Suppose Luther had lost. Then what?"

"He never told me what he'd wagered. I reckon he didn't even *consider* losing. The thing he wanted most in this world was for his family to have a place to call home."

"But a *card* game! I don't know what to think! I have half a mind to give it back."

"Once you're settled on that land, you'll have a good income for life, Mrs. McCann. A sturdy house, and plenty of space to raise your children. It's what Luther wanted."

"A lot of good it does to own land in Texas now," Yancy said. "It could be years before this war ends. Or the Texians could give up their fight for independence. Then the Mexicans would throw out our claim anyway."

146

"Maybe. But General Houston made a speech last week, and he sounded bound and determined to me. After what happened at the Alamo, I don't think the Texians will give up. Not as long as there's a single one of them left standing."

"Meanwhile, we're still here, imposing on Mrs. Franklin," Mama said. "I don't know what we'd have done without her kindness."

"Oh, my blessed," Mrs. Franklin said, blushing. "You and your children have become like family to me. And you're no trouble at all. You and Jessie do more than your share of the work around here."

"That's the truth!" Jessie blurted. "I've swept and polished and washed dishes till my hands are rough as corncobs!"

"Enough, Jessie." Mama turned to Dr. Wilson. "Where will *you* go now?"

"I told General Houston I'd join up with his men, as soon as I made good on my promise to Luther. It's taken me so long to find you, the general's probably given up on me by now." He looked at each of the McCanns in turn. "You can be proud of your pa. He fought for what he believed in, and I never met a man who loved his family more."

Mama and Tad began to weep, but Jessie couldn't cry. It wasn't that she didn't love Pa. She did, despite all he had done to vex her. There was something else stopping her tears, a sick feeling, heavy as lead, around her heart.

147

Mrs. Franklin said to Dr. Wilson, "You're welcome to stay for supper and spend the night."

"I'd be grateful. It's been a while since I've spent so much time in the saddle. I could sleep for a week."

"Well, you just go along now, and set yourself down. You, too, Ruth. I'll have a meal on the table in a little while."

Wiping away her tears, Mama said, "Jessie and I will help you. It's better to keep busy."

Jessie followed them to the kitchen. Dr. Wilson got his medicines from his saddlebags and tended Yancy's shoulder. While she peeled potatoes and set out the serving bowls, Jessie listened to their voices in the next room.

"It's healing slower than I'd like, Yancy, but it is healing," the doctor said. "You're bound to have an ugly scar, though."

"I thought I was going to die out there. A scar seems like nothing." Yancy lowered his voice. "Is it true, what you told Mama about how Pa died?"

Settling down her stack of plates, Jessie pressed her ear to the wall.

"Not exactly," the doctor admitted. "When the shooting started, Luther took off toward the trees. He was hit twice, in the gut. There was nothing I could have done for him, even if the Mexicans had let me. But your poor mother has suffered so much already, it seemed kinder to let her think he went peacefully."

"The truth would kill her," Yancy agreed. "I'm grateful to you, sir."

Jessie heard them start toward the kitchen. She picked up the plates and hurried to the table. She set out the butter crock, poured a pitcher of milk, and helped Mama carry in the serving bowls.

Nobody felt much like eating, but Mama insisted that they try. "We must keep our strength up, and go on hoping for the best."

"I'm hoping Star is still waiting for me when we get home," Tad said.

"Tell you what, Taddie. If we don't find her, I'll get you another cat," Yancy said.

"You will?"

"If Mama says it's all right."

"Can he, Mama?" Tad implored.

"One thing at a time," Mama said. "It's too soon to make any plans, Tad."

When the meal was over, Mrs. Franklin sent everyone to the front porch. "You've had a terrible day," she said. "You rest yourselves and I'll have these dishes finished in no time."

Mama and Dr. Wilson sat in the rocking chairs. Yancy and Tad perched on the porch railing like two thin brown birds. Sitting on the bottom step, Jessie dug her toes into the powdery gray dust, trying not to think about Pa, trying not to feel the guilt spreading over her heart like an ugly stain.

She stole a glance at Yancy. He was the one who listened to all her problems, but she could never confess the awful secret weighing her down.

"Say, Yancy," Dr. Wilson said. "Why don't you get your harmonica and play us a hymn in memory of your pa."

"I lost it on the way to Goliad," Yancy said. "Pa said he'd get me a new one when we got back to San Antonio."

Mama began to sing. " 'I am weak and I am weary . . .' "

" 'But my faith is sure and strong,' " Tad sang.

Jessie made her lips move, but her insides felt as frozen as Hickory Creek in January.

14

ANOTHER JOURNEY

For the next few days, it rained so hard Jessie could scarcely see across the road. Dr. Wilson stayed on at the boardinghouse, waiting for the weather to clear before riding off to join General Houston.

"It's coming a toadstrangler, Mama!" Jessie cried one morning, when a strong wind blew the door open and cold rain poured into the parlor.

"Shut the door, Jess, and help me with the dishes," Mama said.

Jessie sighed. It seemed they were always about to eat, or eating, or cleaning up from eating. And each time, the dirty dishes piled up, tall as the Kentucky mountains. She had just finished drying the last skillet that afternoon when three mud-spattered riders raced down the road, flapping their hats in the air. "Good news!" they shouted. "Good news!"

People spilled out of their houses and onto the road.

Mrs. Franklin bustled to the door, wiping her hands on her apron. "My blessed! What's all the fuss about?"

"General Houston's army has defeated Santa Anna!" one of the riders cried. "The war is over! Texas is free!"

"Yahoo!" Tad jumped up and down. "Is Santa Anna dead? I hope so. I hope General Houston chopped him into a million pieces. I hope they set his ugly uniform on fire. I hope he—"

"Tad," Mama said quietly.

"Well, I do," Tad said. "He deserves it, after what he did to Colonel Travis and Davy Crockett. If it wasn't for him, Pa would still be alive, too."

"How did it happen?" Dr. Wilson asked one of the riders.

"General Houston caught up with Santa Anna on the San Jacinto River. It was seven hundred Texians against fifteen hundred Mexicans. The Texians routed them in eighteen minutes flat and chased them all afternoon, till they finally rounded up General Cós and old Santa Anna himself. He's General Houston's prisoner now."

"That is good news," Dr. Wilson said. "Maybe now we can live in peace."

"Mama, can we go back to San Antonio now?" Tad asked. "I want to find Star."

"She may not be there, Tad," Mama said. "We've been gone a long time. You mustn't be disappointed if we can't find her."

Mrs. Franklin stepped into the road. "Would you

gentlemen like a bite to eat? We've just finished dinner, but there's plenty left over."

"Much obliged, ma'am," said one, wiping the mud from his face, "but we need to push on. Folks in Sabine most likely haven't heard the good news yet. Those that survived the run for the border will be wanting to start home."

"Is it safe to travel?" Mama asked

"General Houston captured most of the Mexicans' guns. I reckon you'll be safe enough if you watch what you're doing."

"Mama," Yancy said. "Surely you're not thinking of going all the way back to San Antonio."

Jessie held her breath. Maybe Mama would decide to stay here in Liberty. Maybe they'd move to New Orleans and she'd see Sarah Austin again.

But Mama said, "Of course we're going back! We're going to live on that farm, just as your pa intended."

"Oh, good!" Tad crowed. "When can we go? Can we leave right now?"

"Slow down, partner," Dr. Wilson said, his expression merry. "It's a long trip. We'll have to make some plans before we head out."

"We?" Mama asked.

He looked sheepish. "I don't know whether you remember, Mrs. McCann, but I came to Texas intending to settle in San Antonio. Now that Santa Anna is defeated, the town is sure to grow. Folks can always use a doctor. I'd consider it an honor if you'd allow me to travel back with you, and see you safely onto your farm."

"Well." Mama wiped her palms on her skirt. "I hardly know what to say."

"Say yes, Mama!" Tad said. "I want to see our farm. I'll bet there's cows and everything."

Jessie glanced at Yancy. He was grinning like a possum, but her heart felt heavy with dread at the mere thought of going back to the place where she'd said such awful things to Pa.

"Yes," Mama said finally. "All right. I'd be much obliged for your help."

The sun was going down behind the trees. The three men wished them luck and rode away. The McCanns and Dr. Wilson returned to the boardinghouse. When Jessie and Tad were ready for bed, Mama sat them down in front of the fire and they said prayers for Pa, and for a safe journey home.

After breakfast the next morning, Dr. Wilson went to the livery to sell his horse and buy a wagon and a team. At Mr. Hollis's store, he bought sugar, flour, coffee, and salt pork. He cleaned his rifle and checked the wagon wheels to be sure none was cracked or loose.

Jessie looked on, amazed at all his clear-headed plans. "He's so . . . orderly," she told Yancy. "Pa would have jumped in the wagon in the middle of the night and we'd have started off with nothing more than the clothes on our backs."

"Pa wasn't much of a planner, that's for sure," Yancy

154

said. "But he did what he thought was right, no matter what anybody else thought." He yanked her braids. "Just like you, Jess."

Mrs. Franklin bustled out to the wagon and handed Mama a box. "Here's a few dishes for you, Ruth. There's some beans and some dried beef to keep you going."

Dr. Wilson helped Mama and Jessie onto the seat. Yancy and Tad sat facing backwards, their legs dangling off the back of the wagon.

"Good-bye, Ruth!" Mrs. Franklin called. "Good luck!"

"Good-bye," Mama said. "Thank you for everything."

Beneath her sun-colored poke bonnet, Mrs. Franklin blushed furiously. "Oh, my blessed. I didn't do much. Jessie, help your mama, you hear?"

"Bye, Mrs. Franklin," Tad said. "When I get home, I'll draw a picture of Star for you."

"You do that," Mrs. Franklin said. "Take care of them, Yancy. You're the man of the family now."

Dr. Wilson released the wagon brake, clicked his tongue to the horses, and the wagon rolled out of the yard. Jessie waved until Mrs. Franklin was just a speck of yellow against the bright blue sky.

The journey seemed endless. Day after day they creaked along the empty countryside toward San Antonio, passing abandoned wagons and broken-down ox carts, and houses and barns standing empty. Sometimes they saw other travelers straggling west along the dry, rutted prairie. Once they saw some graves with nothing more than crude crosses made of sticks, to show where people had died. Jessie hoped someone would make a cross for Pa in the woods at Goliad.

When they made camp each night, Jessie helped Mama make biscuits in the cooking pot. Sometimes, Dr. Wilson shot rabbits and they flavored the meat with wild onions Jessie found growing on the riverbanks. After supper, they sang, or listened to Mama's Bible verses. Sometimes Dr. Wilson told stories. Jessie liked that best of all. He knew funny stories and sad stories and ghost stories so scary they could melt a person's hair clean off his head.

Sometimes the stories were about Pa. When that happened, Jessie saw a special look pass between her mother and the doctor. Once, he held Mama's hand. And just for a minute, the light came back into Mama's eyes again.

Late one afternoon, they camped beside a rushing river. New grass covered the banks and the sun sent pale yellow light flowing along the water. Dr. Wilson halted the wagon and set the brake.

"Yancy, you and Tad take my rifle and see if you can shoot us some supper," he said. "Jessie, I'd be grateful if you'd put some water on. I need a good cup of coffee."

"I'll make it," Mama said.

"No, let Jessie do it. I want to show you something."

He lifted Mama off the wagon, swinging her down carefully, as if she were a china doll. Mama's happy

156

laugh made Jessie's breath catch. Mama was acting exactly like the girls back home when Yancy so much as looked in their direction in church on Sundays. Positively sappy. She scowled.

Tad saw it too. "Yancy?" He squinted up at his brother. "Does Mama love Dr. Wilson?"

Yancy chuckled. "What a question, Taddie."

"Well, does she?"

"Of course she doesn't, you dumb cluck." Jessie banged around inside the wagon, lifting out the cooking pot and the plates. "She loves Pa."

"But Pa's dead."

"Creation!" She threw the pot as hard as she could. It bounced off a tree and rolled into the grass. "Just 'cause somebody's dead don't mean you stop loving them."

Setting down his rifle, Yancy retrieved the pot. "Lordy, what a temper you're in."

He set the pot on the ground, his green eyes steady on hers. "You're almost twelve now, so I reckon you're old enough to understand something. Yes, Mama loved Pa with all her heart, maybe more than he deserved. But the plain truth is, he's gone now. And life is too hard to live all by yourself, Jess. If Ma hooks up with the doctor, it'll be good for both of them. And if I catch you saying or doing anything to break them up, I'll tan your hide myself."

"Will Mama marry him, Yancy?" Tad asked, wide-eyed. "Will we have a new pa?"

"That's for them to figure out. We got nothin' to say about it."

"What if Dr. Wilson wants to kiss her?"

Yancy grinned. "If Mama wants him to, then I reckon he will." He made a fire in the clearing, picked up the rifle, and turned back to Jessie. "Can I trust you not to tear up this camp while Tad and I go hunting?"

Jessie didn't say a word. Yancy jammed his hat on his head. "Go ahead then. Pout if you want to. It won't change a dad-blamed thing. But you better get that water to boiling before Mama and the doctor get back. Come on, Tad. Let's leave Miss Prickle-Britches to herself."

They disappeared into the woods. Jessie stomped down to the river, filled the pot, and set it on the fire. She took out the coffee beans and dumped them in the pot. Then she set out the plates along the back of the wagon.

Soon Mama and Dr. Wilson came up the riverbank, laughing, Mama holding a bouquet of blue and white flowers. She kissed Jessie's cheek. "Thank you for putting the coffee on. I don't know what I'd do without you."

The boys came back through the trees.

"We couldn't find any game, Dr. Wilson," Tad reported.

"Well, don't worry about it. We're almost home, but I was hoping for some fresh meat."

"Me, too." Tad flopped down beside the campfire. "I sure am tired of beans and salt pork."

Dr. Wilson chuckled. "Once you get your farm going, you can have any kind of vegetable you want."

"I don't want vegetables," Tad said. "But I sure wouldn't mind some of Mama's apple pandowdy."

The next morning, they set out once more, the wagon straining up the hills, then rattling down the other side till at last they reached the main road heading west. It was nearly dark when they finally reached San Antonio. The wagon rolled past deserted houses and rumbled across the wooden bridge where Jessie had played with Angelina. It creaked past the inn where Callie had died, past Mrs. Musquiz's adobe house, past the battle-ravaged walls of the Alamo. Jessie's heart was heavy with remembering but she couldn't cry. The hurt went too deep for tears.

At last they came to their cabin at the end of the road. The wagon rolled to a stop in the yard and Dr. Wilson lifted Mama down. Jessie and the boys jumped to the ground. They went up the steps and pushed open the door.

The cabin was full of cobwebs and cloaked in dust. Dr. Wilson lit candles and set them on the mantel. Shadows danced against the walls.

"Mama?" Tad said. "Can I go look for Star?"

"Oh, Tad. You and that cat! I suppose so, but don't be long."

Mama moved slowly around the room, like a person walking in her sleep. She touched Callie's crib, the bare table, the fireplace mantel. "Look," she whispered.

"Your father's favorite tobacco pouch. I can't imagine why he left it behind."

Yancy said, "It's cold in here, Mama. I'll make a fire."

Jessie sat in Pa's chair by the hearth, remembering the night Mr. Atterbury had invited him to join their army. Pa had looked so happy and excited, listening to Yancy play the harmonica. *Dance for me, Jessie.*

"Mama!" Tad burst through the door, his eyes bright as marbles. "Guess what? I found Star! And she's got kittens. Four of them! Under the porch. Come and look."

Mama wiped her eyes. "Five cats, Tad? What on earth will we do with them all?"

"There's plenty of room at our farm, I'll bet. And if there's a barn we'll need lots of cats to keep the mice out, won't we, Dr. Wilson?"

"I don't reckon a person can have too many good barn cats," the doctor said.

"Come on, Mama." Tad yanked on her arm. "They're real cute. They look just like Star."

Yancy came in with an armful of wood. "Let Mama rest a while, Taddie. There'll be time tomorrow to see the kittens."

He lit the fire.

Dr. Wilson said, "I can take you out to your farm tomorrow, if you'd like. Luther said the house is in good shape. There's a cookstove and everything."

"Is there someone to help move our things?"

"I'll ask around. Folks are trickling back in. If we can't find a drayman with a bigger wagon, we'll pile

160

everything onto ours. We'll manage somehow. Will you be all right here tonight?"

"Don't worry about us," Yancy said. "I can take care of my family."

"Yes," Dr. Wilson said. "I can see that. I'm proud of you, boy. Jessie?"

"Sir?"

"Your pa asked me to give you something whenever I thought the time was right. I've been studying on it, and I reckon this is as good a time as any."

Reaching inside his coat, he took out a small leather pouch and opened it into Jessie's palm.

And there, shining in the firelight, was Angelina's silver necklace.

15

A Place to Call Home

"Well, there it is, Ruth. Your farm. Free and clear."
Dr. Wilson jumped from the wagon and helped
Mama and Jessie down. They stood in the shade of the
trees on a rise that gave way to rolling green hills. In the
distance a farmhouse gleamed white in the soft light of
early evening. The pastures were dotted with patches of
creamy clover blossoms, but it was not truly summer
yet. In another month, the trees would be in full leaf
and the hillsides would be full of wildflowers.

Tad stroked Star's head. On the seat beside him, the
kittens slept, curled into an old basket. "All this is
ours?"

"Every last acre," Dr. Wilson said. "I know you'll take
good care of it, the way your pa intended."

Mama shaded her eyes. "Such a large land. It's beautiful, but it seems so empty."

"It won't be empty for long," Dr. Wilson predicted.

"Now that Santa Anna has been defeated, more people will come."

"I wish Pa had lived to see this day," Yancy said. "At night, in the camp, he used to talk about how exciting it would be to build a whole new country."

"I wish Colonel Travis were alive, too," Mama said quietly. "I wish he knew all his efforts, and his terrible death, were not in vain."

"The last time I saw General Houston," Dr. Wilson said, "all he talked about was the Alamo, and how he meant to make Texas safe again. San Jacinto proved he meant it."

"I wish Davy Crockett was still alive," Tad said. "If he knew how General Houston had captured old Santa Anna, he'd laugh his head off."

Yancy stood with his hands on Jessie's shoulders. "Finally, a place to call home. I can hardly believe it."

Jessie clutched Angelina's necklace, barely able to breathe. Right in front of her was everything she'd been waiting for. But instead of feeling happy, she was overcome with sadness. She began to run down the shadowy hillside, along the creek that bordered one edge of the farm. Lifting her skirts, she ran until her lungs screamed for air and she sprawled facedown in the sweet-smelling clover.

In the grass beside her, footsteps stirred, but Jessie didn't move. She couldn't. She was crying so hard her stomach ached, and her throat burned with tears.

"Jessie honey." Mama picked her up, not talking, just

holding on, wiping Jessie's face with the hem of her skirt till the tears finally stopped.

"Better?" Mama brushed back Jessie's tangled braid.

"It's so hard to think of Pa gone forever. And it's all my fault." She felt the tears coming back.

"Nonsense. His luck finally ran out, that's all."

"It is my fault! I told him *he* should have died, instead of Callie. And when you made me apologize, I crossed my fingers so it wouldn't count."

"You were angry at him. But you mustn't blame yourself, Jess. We all say things we don't mean. I imagine that's why Pa sent the necklace back. It was his way of saying he was wrong."

"I was always so mad at him, but I didn't mean for him to die."

"Oh, Jessie. I know that! None of us blames you for what happened."

"I tried hard not to listen to him," Jessie said, "but now I can't forget anything he ever said. It's like he's still alive somehow."

They stood up and Mama took her hand. "The best of a person always lives on, inside the hearts of those they loved. As long as we remember his love of adventure, the music he played, the stories he told, your pa will live on, no matter what happens."

The truth in Mama's words dawned slowly, like a sunrise over the mountains. You could be as good as you knew how to be, and sometimes bad things still happened. But you couldn't let it beat you down. You had to keep going. You had to have hope. That was what Pa had tried to teach her, when she'd been too angry to learn. But she could see it now. She could feel Pa smiling down from heaven, telling her everything was all right, and her heart gave up its heavy burden.

A single star winked on, a tiny blue light in the enveloping darkness. In the whisper of wind in the trees, Pa's voice came to her. *Dance, Jessie. Dance for me.*

There, in the meadow, she danced.

A Brief Texas Chronology

The italicized lines are fictional.

1682 The first Spanish settlement, Ysleta (on the site of present-day El Paso), is established.

1718 Mission San Antonio de Valero, later known as the Alamo, is founded by Franciscan missionaries at San Pedro Springs.

1821 The Spanish government grants Moses Austin permission to establish a colony in Texas, but he dies on the way home.

Mexico gains its independence from Spain after ten years of struggle.

Stephen F. Austin, Moses Austin's son, leads 300 families from the United States to establish a settlement.

1824 Under the new Mexican constitution, Coahuila y Texas becomes a single state.

1830 The Mexican government refuses to allow any further immigration from the United States and also establishes new regulations regarding slavery. But illegal immigration continues.

1832 Colonists from the United States draw up the Turtle Bayou Resolutions, which accuse the government of Mexico of violating the constitution.

Another list of grievances against the Mexican government is drawn up by the United States colonists at a convention in San Felipe de Austin.

1833   Stephen F. Austin presents resolutions to the Mexican government that propose more changes in the local government. The Mexican government grants Texas greater representation in the state legislature.

1834   Antonio López de Santa Anna comes to power in Mexico City.

1835   *October 23. The McCanns begin their journey to Texas.*

November 1. Davy Crockett leaves Memphis, bound for Texas.

November 17. The McCanns arrive in Texas.

December 5–10. The Mexican General Martín Perfecto de Cós is ousted from San Antonio after five days of fighting. Ben Milam is killed in the skirmish.

1836   January 17. General Sam Houston sends Colonel Jim Bowie to the Alamo.

February 2. Colonel William Travis arrives at the Alamo.

February 8. Davy Crockett and his twelve Tennessee boys arrive at the Alamo.

February 23. The siege of the Alamo begins.

March 6. The Alamo falls. The Runaway Scrape begins.

March 27. Colonel James Fannin and his men are massacred at Goliad.

April 13. Angelina arrives in Liberty to lead Jessie to Yancy.

April 21. General Houston defeats General Santa Anna at San Jacinto. General Santa Anna is captured the next day.

May 6. The McCanns return to San Antonio to claim their land.

Author's Note

It has been said that no event in American history is so filled with myth and legend as the siege of the Alamo. Even scholars disagree on almost everything. The timing of its events, the conversations of the participants, the locations and numbers of troops, as well as where, when, and how certain men died, are still debated today. When, many years afterward, the few eyewitnesses finally spoke of their experiences, they gave different accounts of events. To complicate matters further, other people falsely claimed to have been there, claims that were repeated as fact until the line between truth and myth became hopelessly blurred.

Authors of historical fiction must create a blend of what actually happened, what may have happened, and what they imagine could have happened. In writing this story, I relied upon the work of several historians and upon the published letters and diaries of those who were participants in the events. I tried to describe the siege of the Alamo, the Runaway Scrape, and the massacre at Goliad as accurately as possible. Where the opinions of my sources differed, I had to make choices. That is why, when you read other books about this event, you may discover details that are different from those you've just read.

But I also took advantage of poetic license. In this story, the McCanns, the Wyatt Austin family, Jessie's friend Angelina, Dr. Wilson, and Mrs. Franklin are all fictional characters. The defenders of the Alamo—Travis, Bowie, and Crockett—were actual persons, as were Susanna Dickinson, her daughter and husband, the Esparza family, and Mrs. Musquiz.

What should be said of the 182 men who died at the Alamo? Like most real-life heroes, they weren't perfect. They came to Texas with dreams of wealth and power, with dreams of glory, with dreams of adventure. Some were running from the law, some from their complicated pasts. Yet, on that final morning when all hope of victory had evaporated and they had one last chance to flee, they chose to stay and fight, united by their belief in liberty. Today, almost three hundred years after its founding, the Alamo still stands, a reminder of those men, and of the price they paid.